DIVORCE *and* ESTATE PLANNING IN TEXAS

How to Plan Ahead for the Unexpected
and Save Your Family's Future

Laura D. Heard, Esq.

Jacobs & Whitehall
21750 Hardy Oak Blvd
Suite 104
#51700
San Antonio, Texas 78258
www.jacobsandwhitehall.com

Ordering Information:

Quantity sales. Special discounts are available on quantity purchases by corporations, associations, and others. For details, contact the publisher at the address above.

Orders by U.S. trade bookstores and wholesalers. Please contact Jacobs & Whitehall: Tel: (888) 991-2766 or visit www.jacobsandwhitehall.com.

Printed in the United States of America

Published in 2022

ISBN: 978-1-954506-30-5

PREFACE

Divorce and Death - the two big "D's"! Two events that often cause depression and have devastating financial results that can affect not only you but your family too. Downer. Who would want to read a book about that?

But wait! This book is about planning ahead to make things better. Planning can make all the difference in the world. It can literally save your family's future. I have something important to share. After all, we are all going to die someday. Death, and sometimes divorce, may take people by surprise, but these events don't have to bring financial ruin. My purpose is to explain why it is important to talk to an attorney. This book is meant to give you some tools and some vocabulary to know what to do and what to ask when you talk to an attorney. I've even provided a glossary in the back. This book is no substitute for law school and it is not a do-it-yourself manual, but it will bring up some ideas you may never have considered before. Hopefully, this book will help you make sure that nothing important is overlooked. I've tried to include a little bit of something that everyone can use. This book is about real life.

Who knows? If you find this book helpful and share it with a friend, maybe it will become a best-seller. If not, well, if I inspire one person to plan ahead, I will have done some good for that family.

I wish you a long, prosperous life and a long, happy marriage, but I also wish you the peace of mind of knowing you have a plan for every contingency. Whenever in the future you someday die, I want you to leave your loved ones well-prepared. If ever you are faced with divorce, don't let it ruin your plan. This book is a good place to start.

DEDICATION

I dedicate this book to my family, without all of whom I would not be where I am today. Truly I stand on the shoulders of giants.

To: Both of my grandmothers who were career women in an age when that was rare, and who poured their love of creativity into me while showing me that it is possible to balance career and family.

To: My parents who instilled in me a love of education, who sacrificed to send me to college and law school, and who encouraged me to start my own law practice, even though they don't really like lawyers.

To: My husband, John, who has been my Love since middle school, supported my dreams all my life, endured law school with me, started a small business with me, and has been my constant friend, prayer partner, the wind beneath my wings, and my Superman.

And most of all to: Jesus, my Lord and Savior.

PRAISE AND RECOMMENDATION FOR DIVORCE AND ESTATE PLANNING IN TEXAS

"I am excited to recommend Laura Heard's book, *Divorce and Estate Planning in Texas*. Unfortunately, many married people and even their attorneys often overlook the potential of a future divorce when they plan estates. This failure can cause tremendous difficulties to both partners, their children, other family members, and even friends ... Laura's book does a fantastic job of explaining what every married person should consider when crafting his or her estate plan, in easy-to-understand language and with a conversational tone that makes her book both an enlightening and enjoyable read."

Dr. Gerry W. Beyer
Governor Preston E. Smith Regents Professor of Law
Texas Tech University School of Law

DISCLAIMER

This publication is intended to be used for educational purposes only. No legal advice is being given, and no attorney-client relationship is intended to be created by reading this material. Remember that the law is constantly changing and it is not the same in every State. The author assumes no liability for any errors or omissions or for how this book or its contents are used or interpreted, or for any consequences resulting directly or indirectly from the use of this book. For legal or any other advice, please consult an experienced attorney or the appropriate expert, who is aware of the specific facts of your case and is knowledgeable in the current law in your jurisdiction.

Laura D. Heard Law Firm, Inc.
14607 San Pedro Ave.,
Suite 205
San Antonio, TX 78232
(210) 655-9090
www.ldheard.com

Testimonials

"I called other law offices before deciding on the L.D. Heard Law Firm. From my first meeting in their office, I knew I had made the right decision. Laura Heard explained the legal process to me and showed genuine concern for me. Her assistants are knowledgeable and very personable. Laura has kept me informed on all developments and answered my questions promptly. I know she has other cases, but she handles my case as if it were her only one. I would recommend this law firm to anyone needing any family law matters resolved."

– C. Davis

****

*"I was actually referred to Laura by a man who said Laura represented his ex-wife and **she 'beat the pants off of him in court.'** Laura and her team have been great in keeping me informed about the status of my divorce and she made making a Will easy too."*

– Tammy F.

****

"I have known Laura for over 25 years. She is a consummate professional but her most outstanding characteristic is her high moral and ethical standards. I live in Fort Worth but chose to use someone I knew and trusted for my legal services. Laura is a very warm and caring person and I highly recommend her to anyone needing legal services."

– bjchester

****

"Laura Heard was my husband's attorney in my divorce. I thought I had a good attorney, but [my attorney] he gave Laura everything she wanted. After she took my deposition, I knew I had lost. Now I refer all my friends to Laura Heard, not to the attorney I used. Laura Heard has done a good job for everyone I sent to her."

– ida-now

****

"Laura continues to be a great counselor. She is responsive, caring, and leads her clients thru difficult situations for the best possible outcome. Highly recommend."

- Mike

****

"Laura and her team helped me settle the estate of my mother. She was available and did an excellent job for me. Laura and team are professional but friendly and made me feel confident and in safe hands."

– Anonymous

****

"I would like to say that Laura is an AWESOME attorney. I really agree with her response … some people are going to make things up in an attempt to hurt an attorney. I would recommend Laura to everyone I know. If you are looking for a good attorney, take advantage of her consultation; it will make your decision making much easier. She truly is great."

- Matt H.

****

"I highly recommend Laura Heard as a family practice attorney!!! She specializes in divorce, child custody and child abuse cases, as well as probate law. I have never known someone who works from such a solid faith foundation which gives her the empathy that many attorneys lack, along with 34 years of solid experience and expertise! Quite simply, she is the best!"

– Karen Gallagher

****

"My husband and I recently had our wills and powers of attorney (durable and medical) written by Laura Heard. She was the best: professional, friendly, and knowledgeable. Laura helped us navigate through all of the options to make our wills reflect our wishes, answered our many questions, and talked us through some issues with estate planning. I will definitely go to her again with any Family Law issues I might have in the future, and I wholeheartedly recommend Laura Heard to anyone needing a Family Law attorney."

–Elizabeth S.

****

"Laura has given us invaluable guidance for many years as our family attorney. Laura has taken our concerns and questions seriously, advising us on a detailed plan, tailored to us.... Laura's integrity, unwavering devotion to God, compassion, and her dedication to serve make her the only choice for our family. Laura is also an amazing advocate for abused and foster children. She's not just their attorney, she truly cares for these children and becomes their friend."

-- C. Neill

****

"Laura Heard is the most kind and compassionate lawyer. She assisted me with my divorce as well as my Will. She and her staff were with me every step of the way. She has years of wisdom and seniority that I needed and it really contributed to being able to re-establish me and helped rebuild our lives. She will be very responsive and straightforward with her client and you are not left wondering if there is anything that has been overlooked. Her staff is exemplary, and her work ethic is the best of the best. She is truly gifted in her calling and it really makes a difference with clear communication. She is worth the investment. She truly cares and is intentional and does not waste money or time. She has integrity and has won multiple awards!"

—Kathryn Taylor

****

"Attorney Laura Heard is a professional, knowledgeable, and compassionate family lawyer. Laura is a member of our church so my husband and I turned to her for an update on our trust and to have some technical things handled for the trust. Laura was thorough and able to call to our attention things we overlooked before finalizing it. Later, my mother desired to update her trust and her will. I recommended that she see Laura. Again, Laura pointed out things that should be addressed that mom did not consider. Laura updated my mother's trust a second time and now Laura is helping me handle my mom's estate after her passing."

—Diane Dawsey

****

For more current reviews, Google:
"Laura D. Heard Law Firm"

TABLE OF CONTENTS

Section III What If We Don't Plan Ahead?

About The Author

When I became an attorney, I took an oath to support the law and to represent my clients with honesty and integrity. I take that oath seriously to this day. I have been blessed to be born in Texas and privileged to have a very long career in both family law and probate law in Texas. I went to law school to study estate planning and probate, and writing has long been a passion of mine, hence this book on the topics that I think everyone needs to know. Family law and probate are the areas of law that will affect most ordinary people at some point.

This may come as a surprise, but in most Texas counties other than the largest ones, there aren't separate Probate Courts. Instead, probate usually gets handled in a section of a wider-use county court. Bexar County, on the other hand, which encompasses San Antonio, currently has two Probate Courts that do nothing but probate and related matters. Probate includes not only the estates of deceased persons, but also guardianships for people of all ages, and surprisingly, the statutory probate court has the power to pull in a divorce or paternity case that is related to the probate or guardianship, even the power to take it away from District Court.

The very first probate judges to sit on the benches of the Bexar County Probate Courts were appointed around the time that I was in law school. I have, therefore, known and practiced before every single judge who has ever sat on the bench of any Probate Court in Bexar County. Not too many attorneys can say that. In addition, while based in San Antonio, I've enjoyed handling cases all over the State of Texas.

During law school, I was privileged to work for Dr. Gerry Beyer, one of the finest and most respected professors of probate law in Texas. I helped Dr. Beyer write a textbook for law students on probate and wills, as well as a form book for attorneys on estate administration, wills, and probate. I will be forever grateful for that experience. In 1986, I was thrilled to publish my first article as a solo author on a probate law topic in St. Mary's Law Journal ("A Time to be Born, A Time to Die: Alternative Reproduction and Texas Probate Law," by Laura D. Heard, 17 St. Mary's Law Journal 927 (1986)).

In law school, I also studied divorce law and was very interested and invested in it: in fact, I earned the highest grade among everyone in my law school class on the topic of family law that semester. Later I learned that the majority of cases heard in civil District Courts are family law cases. In general, family law lawyers spend more time in contested hearings in the courtroom than any other lawyers. (Move over, Perry Mason and Matlock!)

My legal and writing education continued when I was honored to be chosen as a briefing attorney for the Fourth Court of Appeals in San Antonio in 1987-1988.

When I started my practice of law, I began to realize how much overlap there is between the Texas Estates Code and the Family Code, both in terms of property and children. When it comes down to it, both are largely concerned with dividing community property in Texas and both concern family relationships. I have always been fascinated with that intersection in family law and probate cases. You will see evidence of that overlap between probate and family law/divorce throughout this book.

In the year 2000, I began receiving appointments to Child Protective Services cases, helping children who had been removed from their parents because of abuse and neglect. The bright spot in that area of law is when an adoption takes place.

Now, my practice is equally focused on family law and probate, and whenever I talk about one area of the law, I always think about the implications for the other, and it surprises me that other lawyers don't see the two areas as intricately intertwined. While I spend a great deal of my time sorting and dividing up property for people in estate planning, divorce, inheritances, or mediation, I am surprised to find that many estate planning attorneys shy away from any divorce case and many family law attorneys refuse to do anything related to Wills or probate. Not to mention the majority of attorneys who would never touch a child abuse case or handle a protective order.

I feel that because of my varied experiences, my law firm is really able to offer a full spectrum of legal services, from the cradle to the grave. My firm helps people with legal issues from adoptions, pre and post-nuptials, divorce, retirement and real estate divisions, child custody, child support, and child abuse to estate planning and setting up trusts, and finally to the probate of estates after death, with and without a Will.

I have been practicing that way and offering that range of services since 1987. I love the fact that since then, I have been privileged to hear people's life stories every day, some of them quite amazing and inspirational. Often, my work puts me in the position to help people through the worst times in their lives. I feel honored to be able to regularly serve as a sympathetic ear for people who are really at a low point, and also to encourage them and help them make their lives better for the future. That is a part of my job that I absolutely love.

My motto has become "Justice Flows from Truth, Compassion, Wisdom, and Persistence."™ My goal is to help provide peace for people who are suffering great stress due to divorce or death of a loved one.

Who Are You Writing This Book For?

I'm writing this book to encourage people to plan ahead, no matter what your stage in life.

Often, we're so caught up in the moment and overwhelmed with life as it happens that we can't think about—or prepare for—the things that will be most important in the future. If a person is in a rocky marriage that they know is headed downhill, they need to be planning ahead for the possibility of divorce. They need to stop doing what most people do, which is just waiting until they get served with divorce papers and then finding themselves completely overwhelmed with no plan or preparation in place. Like the old story of the frog in boiling water, they don't feel things getting hotter and hotter. I know many people are in denial and hope things will get better, and sometimes one spouse is completely unaware that the other is having an affair and planning to leave. Sometimes it is the grandparents who find themselves unexpectedly raising their grandchildren.

It never hurts to have some basic understanding of legal concepts of divorce and child custody just in case, if not for you, then for a friend you may be able to help. Life is messy and divorce is complicated.

The same goes for people who do not have a will. Put bluntly, you never know when you're going to die. Everyone tends to think of death as something that will happen sometime way off in the future. Sometimes they're right, but unfortunately, it doesn't always work out that way. Recently, I wrote a Will for a man who is 99 years old and never had a will before. He had just decided that maybe he didn't have too much longer left in this life. But children and healthy young adults die every day. Car accidents happen all the time, as do heart attacks. Neither are usually planned for, and both often catch people completely unprepared. Young healthy people get killed in accidents, and COVID-19 has taken millions of people in the last two years. Sudden death simply highlights the fact that there is so much we cannot know about when and where our lives will end. Death is not merely for the elderly. Death comes to people regardless of their intelligence, health, age, race, gender, or economic status.

The only thing you do know is that death will happen to all of us eventually and that it makes a big difference to the people you leave behind if you have planned ahead. A big difference. Young people, old people, single people, married people, divorced people, rich people, poor people ... everyone needs this book.

Isn't Planning Ahead Much Kinder Than Leaving Your Loved Ones In The Lurch?

Absolutely. When someone dies without having done any planning, managing their estate is so much more expensive, time consuming, and overwhelming. I can tell you this from experience as someone who has managed many different types of estates: managing the estate of someone who left no will is much more difficult than managing the estate of someone who had a will put together in advance by a qualified estate planning attorney in their home state.

Importantly, I do not say this for my benefit. I have heard people claim that estate planning attorneys only stress the importance of leaving a will because they want to make money by writing the wills and billing for the estate planning hours. Really, though, the opposite is true. I tend to make far more money untangling the estates of people who do not leave wills behind than I make working on the estates of those who do. This is largely because, as mentioned earlier, managing an estate without a will requires far more work, effort, and time. I've seen the tragic results of a probate matter that could have been so different with a simple will. I stress the importance of estate planning not to line my own pockets, but rather because I want people to know how to do the best thing for their loved ones.

When it comes to end-of-life planning, the best thing a person can do for their loved ones is to leave a will and/or an estate plan. The plan should be written by, or at least checked by, an attorney to make sure that it will work. Just because it makes sense to you does not mean it will stand up in court.

With professional assistance, writing a Will doesn't have to be difficult. The task is so often put off because people don't know what they want it to say, but an attorney can help with that. There's an old saying that the best time to plant a tree was ten years ago. The second best time to plant a tree is today. Just get a basic plan in place and then improve on it over time.

Is It True That Estate Planning Is A Life-Long Process?

Yes, it is true that estate planning is an ongoing process that you can participate in during different stages of your life. Estate planning should be a process that occurs over time, and you should update from time-to-time, but you should not wait until you are old to make a Will. Wills should change as the circumstances of a person's life change.

Younger people (especially if they are single with no children) often believe that wills aren't for them. They argue that they don't really have any assets or anyone to account for, since they're still building the foundation for their lives and are just getting started in their careers.

However, when you really think about it, young people have plenty of assets—just different assets than older people tend to have. If you are young and single, it doesn't mean that you don't need a will. It just means that you need a will that concerns itself with issues and assets that pertain to you. If there are matters to be settled, then you need to name an executor to settle those matters. Also, if a young person is killed in a manner that gives rise to a lawsuit, such as a car or construction accident, or on the job, or due to medical malpractice, someone needs to have the authority to file that wrongful death suit and collect the damages on behalf of the estate. That is an executor's job.

Wills for people in the younger, single demographic tend to focus on issues such as:

- Who will inherit the money in the person's bank accounts?
- Who will inherit the person's vehicle or their other high-value belongings?
- What will happen to the person's sentimental objects, and what will happen to their pets (if any)?
- Who will inherit the person's final paycheck or the beginnings of their 401k from work?
- What if the person is due to receive an income tax refund? Who can file the final tax return?
- Who gets the return of the security deposit on the deceased person's apartment or any other refunds that are due to be collected?

Even if a young person doesn't have all of those assets, the point remains that everybody has something that they want to make sure the right person ends up with after they are gone. Without a Will, unfortunately, sometimes it would cost more in attorney's fees to recover a small bank account than the money that is in the account. In those cases, the bank will eventually turn the money over to the government as abandoned property simply because there was no way for the family to get the money without an expensive court order.

There is something called a "Small Estate Affidavit," but that is not the quick fix that people expect it to be. The Small Estate Affidavit has a very limited application and many estates with very few assets still do not qualify. Attorneys may creatively come up with some "band-aid" fixes to help as much as possible after a person has died without a Will, but in every case, a Will would have been better, more efficient, and less costly.

As you get older, your life often changes. If you have children, your will needs to be reworked fundamentally to reflect that fact. Minor children are often the primary concern of their parents' wills, both in terms of inheritance and in terms of who would take guardianship of the children if anything happens to the parents.

Picking a guardian is a very serious matter: they must be very carefully selected after dedicated consideration. If both you and your child's other parent die, their guardian becomes responsible for raising them until they are of age, and also for managing any property, money, or other assets you leave to them (as minor children cannot legally manage their own inheritance until they turn 18).

Then, as you continue to get older, your life continues to change. Once your children grow up and become adults, you will be less concerned with who would be their guardian in the event of your death, and more concerned with who would be your guardian in the event of your incapacity. Your estate planning at that point in life has to do with deciding who you trust to represent your best interests and protect you if you cannot do so yourself. It also has to do with the questions most people commonly think of when they think of estate planning: that is, decisions regarding who gets which assets from an older person's estate which the older person has accrued over the course of their long lifetime. Many older people own a home or other real estate, as well as have some type of retirement income.

At that stage in life, estate planning can involve some extremely intimate, sensitive questions. Do you trust your children (or, at least one of your children) to act as your guardian or to inherit your assets, or do you want to name someone else? Do you want or need a document that specifically excludes certain people from taking guardianship? Do you want or need to do the same for asset inheritance? These questions are often complicated by the relationships of blended families and second marriages as we will discuss later.

Another change to consider in estate planning as a person goes through different stages in life is concern about taxes. As people get older, they usually accumulate more assets, and the total size of their estate usually grows. As that happens, people need to think about whether their estate has become large enough to qualify for an estate tax. If it has, they need to think about the best or most effective way to avoid estate taxes.

The rules of the estate tax, just like all laws, change over time so you need a lawyer who knows the current laws. Even though your Will or estate plan may have been good when it was written, it might no longer be good today. The only law that counts is the law in effect on the date of your death.

So you see, as life continues, your assets change, your family grows and shrinks, your children become adults, you may get divorced and remarried, you may find yourself raising your grandchildren, you may move to a different state, and each of those things may cause you to need to revise your estate plan.

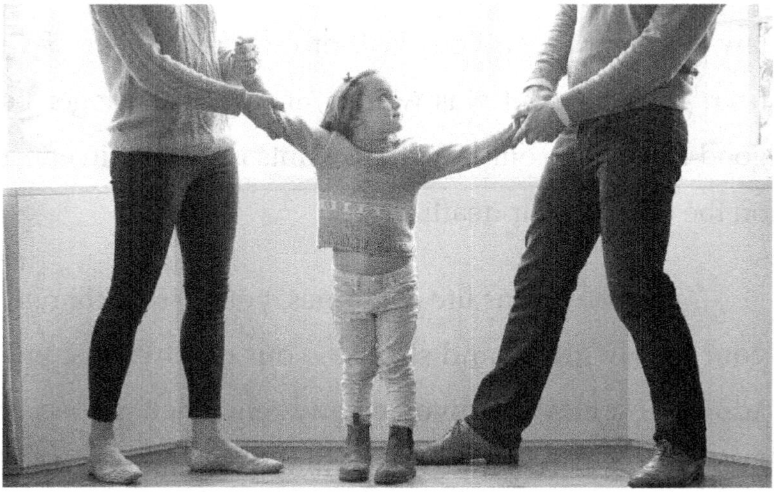

SECTION I
DIVORCE

CHAPTER 1

OPTIONS FOR DIVORCE IN TEXAS

When a marriage fails in Texas, you're either married or you're divorced. There's really no option in between. When you decide you want to get divorced, you file a petition for divorce and start a process that takes perhaps a year or two (during which the divorce is "pending" but you are still officially as married as you were before you filed for divorce). At the end of that process, the matter in court is resolved, and the divorce is finalized when a judge signs an Order called a "Final Decree of Divorce."

In Texas, we don't have the framework usually known as "legal separation," which is common in many other states. This construct used in other states essentially allows for a "waiting period" during which you are no longer legally married but are not yet legally divorced, and the separation affects the legal ownership of property. Currently, Texas has a 60-day waiting period from the time you file the original petition until the date that the Judge can sign the final decree of divorce, which is a shorter waiting period than in many other states, but until the judge signs the final decree, the separation makes no legal difference.

It is not uncommon for a person to come to me seeking a divorce when their marriage failed many years before and the parties have lived totally separate lives for sometimes decades. Nevertheless, in Texas, we consider the couple legally married even though they are separated. Since they are never legally divorced, they are still married, and that means that all the property acquired in that period of separation is still community property which the judge must divide. Further, community property is liable to pay debts incurred during the marriage even though one party had no idea what the other was doing. It often is an unpleasant surprise when one spouse has worked hard and accumulated assets and now finds that half of their current assets, including retirement funds, are awarded to the spouse they haven't seen in decades. If a person in that situation dies leaving a Will which gives all their property to their new significant other, the new boyfriend or girlfriend will only get half the community property and the other half will go to the estranged spouse, in spite of the Will.

As a married couple, they have equal rights to their community property and their kids, even though a divorce suit has started. As such, Temporary Orders hearings are often necessary. In many cases, temporary orders are the only legally enforceable way to figure out the details of what life will look like between the time you file for divorce and the time the divorce is finalized (i.e., who is going to pay which bills, who gets to live in the house, sometimes ordering the house sold, setting temporary child support, custody, holidays and visitation rules). Temporary orders hearings give the parties space to advocate for their needs and request all necessary orders that will be enforceable by the Court as they work out the terms of the divorce pre-finalization.

However, the fact remains that the litigated contested divorce process in Texas usually takes 1-2 years, sometimes longer, and if a person were to die in the middle of that process, then they would still officially be married upon their death, and the divorce suit will be dismissed as if it never happened. This poses significant issues for the reasons already mentioned. If you want to try to avoid that issue, Texas does have the option of trying to mediate the case, which can help to significantly speed up the process as well as providing other advantages.

Mediation

Mediation is a process whereby a neutral third party facilitates a settlement discussion in a confidential, informal, and non-confrontational setting. It is a kinder and gentler way of settling disputes than a contested trial and often has better results because the Judge in a contested trial does not have the legal ability nor the time to listen to all the facts, but the parties may work out a solution themselves that the law would not have given them. Only the parties know all the true facts and reasons why they may want certain outcomes, and although lawyers may present evidence in court, some evidence simply cannot be introduced in court under our rules of evidence. For example, while the law may only permit alimony to last for five years, the parties may have a reason to agree to make it last longer. Often there are embarrassing facts that neither party wants to be heard in the public forum of a courtroom. Once that agreement for all the necessary elements of a divorce is put into a written mediated settlement agreement, it will be enforced by the courts. A divorce decree must still be signed, but the judge will not contradict the Mediated Settlement Agreement.

Many Texas counties have local rules that require all contested divorce cases involving children to be mediated before a trial is allowed, particularly any jury trial. Even when the parties both think there is no way the case can be settled, most mediations are successful.

The mediator never decides the final outcome, so if the parties cannot agree, they can still take the dispute to court. The mediator cannot be called to testify, and the parties cannot testify about what was said in mediation if the case did not settle. I am a mediator who is specially trained to handle family law mediations, and I have successfully settled many cases in mediation, including all types of family law, divorce, child custody, guardianship, contested adoptions, and probate matters. Countless times I've heard my clients say that mediation won't work because the other side will not be reasonable, but then the mediation does work at least 80-90% of the time.

One of the methods of mediation is a concept called "collaborative law", in which both sides try to approach their mutual issues less as adversaries and more as two parties trying to come to a solution that is as mutually beneficial as possible.

As an example of collaborative law, consider the following scenario. Say a divorcing couple has many investments and assets that need to be split between them, and in order to do so, those investments and assets need to be evaluated by an expert who appraises real estate and businesses. Small businesses can be difficult to put a value on. Sometimes an accountant is required to evaluate how much of the property is community property and how much is separate property. Applying the collaborative law approach would mean both parties agree to have one mutually-agreed-upon expert conducting the evaluation in each area (accounting, investments, appraisers, sometimes even child psychology), rather than both parties hiring their own separate evaluators. Having a single expert that both sides trust, rather than competing experts, creates much less of an adversarial situation. It also saves time, money, and stress, and expedites the overall process.

It should be noted that in order to successfully pull off a collaborative law approach to divorce, there must be at least some trust between the divorcing parties. Both parties have to be fairly confident that the other party is not hiding assets or debts. The couple also needs to have the available funds to have several experts involved in the divorce, since collaborative law tends to use a team of specialists to help with mediation.

If those conditions are met, collaborative law will likely facilitate a much quicker and easier divorce process at the end of the day, and one that is better tailored to your particular situation.

Putting your contested case before a judge is the last resort in collaborative law cases, particularly since the issues are complicated and judges do not have time to hear all the evidence. Most collaborative cases get settled before you get to the courtroom judge stage, one way or the other, whether by an informal agreement or through a mediator.

While each party has a lawyer to advise them and assist with the legal documents necessary to complete the divorce and divide the property, part of the contractual agreement in collaborative cases is that those lawyers who are assisting in the collaborative process will not litigate the case. If the case cannot be settled, then both parties must fire their attorneys and hire new ones for the litigation. Neither party is allowed to keep the attorney that participated in the collaborative process.

In my experience, mediation—especially collaborative law mediation—is often pursued by couples who want to get the process over with and are more or less already willing to approach the situation cooperatively. In fact, some couples will even start the mediation process before they officially file for divorce. This pre-emptive mediation usually helps them work a vision for the future that is at least relatively mutually agreeable.

Post-Divorce Teams

Post-divorce, those cases that involve extensive property often require a team to help the client with their new start in life. The lawyer may be involved in preparing retirement division orders and communicating with the former spouse's employer about dividing the 401(k) or pension, and withholding wages for alimony/spousal maintenance or child support. There is often a need for a realtor to sell real estate, and the lawyer may assist with advising the client on the paperwork necessary to sell a house. Many people benefit from a financial advisor, stockbroker, career counselor, insurance agent, and other experts to help them invest and protect their assets. Each professional has their own field of expertise. It may be especially helpful to have the advice of a financial expert who can assist with the property division in terms of tax laws and stock values. If the client needs liquidity, a settlement that is primarily retirement funds that they cannot use for many years without heavy fees and taxes may not be a good settlement, even if the dollar value appears to be a great deal on paper. Sometimes, the person who really wants to keep the house, really cannot afford to keep the house, and they need to know that before they give up everything else in the settlement process in order to get a house that they cannot afford to keep. This emotional time is a time when the parties need to get some objective advice.

Even when ending a bad or abusive marriage, at least one of the parties may experience grief, similar to mourning a death, when the divorce is all finished. There are grief counselors who can help, and divorce recovery support groups may be found online or at the local church.

CHAPTER 2

DIVISION OF ASSETS AND DEBTS IN DIVORCE

Generally, as attorneys working on divorce and division of assets cases, we like to create a spreadsheet. We put all the couple's assets and debts on the sheet as numerical values. Then we try to equalize the equations, such that the bottom line is more or less a 50/50 division of the whole net estate.

In some cases, this method may mean that one party gets more debts, but they also get more assets.

However, balancing the books on these cases is kind of like doing a puzzle. You can move the pieces around in many different ways for approximately the same bottom line.

This is helpful because of the emotional aspects people attach to various assets and debts. Some things that have relatively low monetary value, have a great deal of sentimental or emotional baggage value, and a person going through divorce might be willing to give up a great deal more property than that item is worth in order to keep it or in order to make the other person take it. Other times although all community property is liable to pay for a debt incurred during the marriage, one spouse may be loath to pay any part of that debt because of what it represents. For example, a wife may not want to pay a credit card bill that the husband used to pay for gifts and hotel rooms during his affair.

Family law attorneys have all stories of clients who spent thousands of dollars in attorney's fees arguing over possession of some insignificant asset such as a toaster or rolling pin. (I'm not just making this up – these are actually the objects of lengthy court battles). This phenomenon also frequently occurs in probate cases where family members fight over seemingly insignificant items that belonged to the deceased, not because of intrinsic value but because of what the item represents emotionally.

Importantly, we don't just go through and split every debt in half and say, "Husband: you pay half of this debt, and Wife: you pay half of the same debt." To do that would be to make the divorcing spouses remain financial partners for years to come. Instead, each debt is usually assigned to the person whose name is on that debt as the responsible party with the lender. For example, if one party took out a credit card in their name, they will likely be assigned primary responsibility for debt attached to that credit card. This is largely because the creditor is going to go after that person in case of default, since the debt is attached to their name. If you assign the Wife's debt to the Husband and the Husband doesn't pay it, even with the court order, the default will not harm the credit of the Husband. Thus, he has little incentive to pay it. It will still only harm the person who originally signed for the debt, even though the court order says they are not responsible. The Wife will be getting all the nasty collection calls. Even worse, if the debt is tied to some collateral, such as a vehicle or house that item could get foreclosed upon or repossessed if the party not in possession of the collateral does not pay the debt. The only recourse for the Wife is to file a suit to enforce against the former spouse who was ordered to pay.

We sometimes have to get creative in paying off joint debts with joint assets, so that you don't end up with a couple having a continued business relationship for many years after divorce as they try to pay off joint debt.

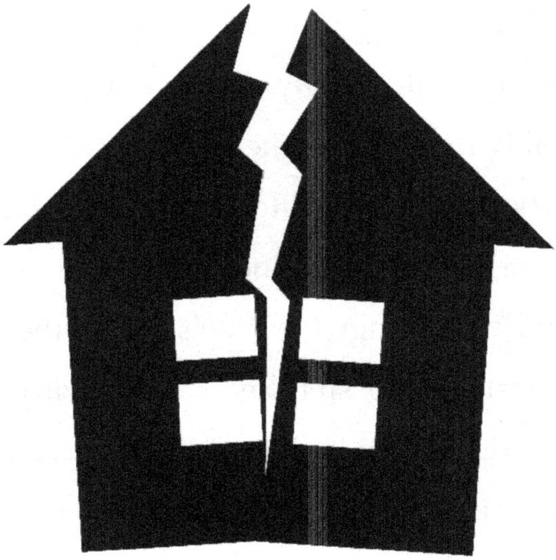

For instance, a shared house is usually a couple's biggest asset or biggest investment. If a divorcing couple bought a house during their marriage, there are several different ways that they can handle the division of that asset, whether the house is kept by one of the parties or sold.

Common options for divorcing couples in this situation include:

- Selling the house and dividing the proceeds between the two parties which will both divide equity and resolve the issue of the joint debt.

- One party staying in the house and refinancing. In this case, the party who stays can do a cash-out refinance and pay off the other party's half of the equity, or they can do a promissory note and continue making incremental payments to the other party over a period of time in order to pay off the equity.
- One party staying in the house with the children until they grow up, and then selling the house. If a divorcing couple decides to go this route, they need to get the house appraised or agree on the value at the time of divorce and award the house to the appropriate party, so that the other party is not continuing to get the benefit of the increased equity in the house that only one party is paying for after the divorce.

There are other large community assets that also need to be divided in a divorce. Cars are a good example, as are boats and other vehicles. Generally, if you award one party a car or vehicle, they get the debt that goes along with that vehicle as well. This is not always the case and depends on the situation and the discretion of the judge. However, it is certainly a trend.

CHAPTER 3

HOW IS CHILD CUSTODY DETERMINED IN TEXAS?

Texas has gender-neutral laws, which means that judges deciding custody matters are not supposed to favor either parent. There are still some older Family Court judges who seem to favor mothers over fathers, but it's ultimately up to the attorneys to be persuasive as to which parent should hold primary custody. The judges can tell when a party merely wants custody to avoid paying child support. I have been successful many times to win custody for a father who truly was the primary caretaker of the children before the marriage fell apart. Those situations are almost always nasty and expensive fights.

Texas law presumes that all parents are fit parents unless proven otherwise and that all parents should be "joint managing conservators," unless there is evidence that joint managing is not in the child's best interests. The parent who has the primary right to determine where the child lives is the one we usually refer to as the one with "primary" custody. However, it has become normal to impose a geographical restriction so that the parent who decides where the child lives must stay within a certain geographic area (such as Bexar County and those counties that touch Bexar County or even restricted within a certain school district). That does not mean they can never travel outside that boundary, say for a vacation or a wedding, but they cannot move the child's primary residence from that area unless the other parent moves out of the area.

Often, custody is decided based on the *status quo* in the child's life. If one parent had been acting de-facto as the child's primary parent before the divorce, that parent is more likely to get primary custody after the divorce. Still, though, the ultimate goal—if possible—is to split parenting and custody duties 50/50. Sometimes, particularly in temporary orders, the judge will not give either parent the right to determine where the child lives but will order that the child stays in a certain school district and if either parent moves out of the school district, the child will stay with the parent who remains living in that district.

The public policy in Texas is to encourage a relationship between the children and both parents, even if one of the parents was not very involved with the child previously. While one parent may prefer that the other parent's visits be limited or supervised, the courts are hesitant to do that, and when they do, it is generally only for a short period of time and with solid evidence of good cause.

Texas also presumes that the children should be kept together. There are cases when it makes sense to place one child with one parent, and the sibling with the other parent, but it is generally frowned upon. The presumption is that it is in the children's best interests to stay together, but particularly in blended families, that is not always possible.

One misconception is that at some age the children get to decide whether to visit the non-custodial parent or which parent they want to be primary. That is never true before the age of 18. Currently, if a child who is at least 12 years of age wishes to express to the judge which parent they prefer to have primary custody, the judge must *listen* to (have a conversation with) the child. However, the judge does not have to do what the child wants done. Judges are trained and attuned to listen for signs that a child has been coached in what to say. It is true that once a child reaches age 16 or 17, particularly if they have a driver's license, then the judge is more likely to allow the child's desires to control visitation, but it is ultimately up to the judge. Whatever the Order says must be followed, even if the child does not want to go to the visit. A parent can be held in contempt of court, and even jailed, for refusing to turn over a child when it is time for the other parent to have possession.

Saying the child didn't want to go, is not a defense. Rather than jail time, however, many times a judge will impose what may be considered a harsher penalty by changing custody. The judge can give the non-custodial parent primary possession of the child to make up for the other parent's reluctance to enforce visitation.

It is always important to remember that family law in Texas is constantly changing and judicial trends change too. The Texas Legislature meets every two years, and every time they meet, they change something in the Texas Family Code. They're always tweaking the laws around child support, child custody arrangements, visitation standards, and other parts of family laws that apply throughout the state. Sometimes the laws and policies get changed a little, and sometimes they get a major overhaul, but every two years, some parts of the Family Code get changed.

Take visitation laws, for example. As it stands, "standard visitation" is the first, third, and fifth weekend of every month. (Attorneys and judges don't like the word "visits" by the way, but prefer to call it "periods of possession" as in the statute.) The timing of each visit used to be from Friday at 6 pm to Sunday at 6 pm. Then the law changed, and we started what is called the "extended standard visitation" schedule, in which each visit starts from the time school lets out on Friday and lasts until the time school starts again on Monday morning. Then extended standard became standard for parents who live within 50 miles of each other.

These days, more and more couples are abandoning "standard visitation" and adopting other schedules to even out the time between the parents. A few years ago, the judges were reluctant to vary from the standard schedule, and they would worry about whether it might make the child's life too unstable, but these alternative and creative plans were necessary when parents worked in shifts or every weekend. Now, these alternative schedules are much more accepted.

One popular arrangement is "one week on, one week off", or two weeks on and two weeks off. There's another scheme called "2/2/3", where one parent (A) has Monday and Tuesday (2 days), then the other (B) has Wednesday, Thursday, (2 days), back to the first parent

(A) on the weekend Friday to Sunday (3 days) one week, and the next week it is reversed to favor the other parent (B gets the next weekend). There are even plans called "2/2/5/5" and "4/3/3/4." One wonders how the parents keep the schedules straight, but there are phone apps to help. These are all different attempts to equalize the time between the mother, the father, and the kids.

Some of the arrangements families think of are more outside the box than others. For instance, there's one arrangement called "nesting" where the children stay in the house and both parents have their own apartments. The parents switch off staying in the house with the children. One week, the mom will live in the house with the children and the dad will live in his own apartment, and the next week, the arrangement will be reversed. The idea behind nesting is that the parents are the ones who are constantly moving in and out of the house instead of the children.

In this way, Texas is the state of creativity. You can customize your child support and child visitation arrangements in virtually any way that makes sense to both parties and does not harm the wellbeing of the children. Mediation allows for families to be especially creative. As long as the parents are relatively good at co-parenting and communicating when it comes to their kids, they can do just about anything by agreement. And even when there is a court-ordered visitation schedule, the courts want the parents to be flexible and accommodate each other for temporary changes in scheduling by agreement.

Of course, there are also situations where parents don't communicate at all. Those are more difficult cases, but it is still my job to try to guide those parents in co-parenting their children. Sometimes, though, I find that it is helpful to bring in a counselor or family therapist, who can help me facilitate dialogue to ultimately reach an agreement, and they may continue to assist after the divorce is final. Usually, the family therapist or co-parenting coach has an hourly rate that is less expensive than the attorney's rate. Alternatively, sometimes a court orders a separate attorney to represent the children, at the expense of one or both parents. I have often served as the children's attorney.

It is important for parents to remember that children identify with both of their parents, as a part of who the child is and becomes. If one parent is constantly tearing down and criticizing the other parent, the child takes that personally and the child's self-esteem is affected. I've represented hundreds of children in child abuse cases where the children are removed from their parents and placed in foster care or with a relative. No matter how bad their living conditions were prior to removal, when the child reaches age 18 and is able to make their own decisions, they nearly always want to re-establish a relationship with their parent. Children love the most unlovable parents sometimes. Trying to convince a child that their other parent is not worthy of love will most often backfire on the parent who tries it. The best strategy is to never talk about one's frustrations or anger at the other parent when the children can overhear you. Your children did not choose their parents, nor did they choose the divorce, and they are not your counselors nor confidants. Your job is to shield them and take care of their emotional needs. They may be very mature, but they are not adults, and the upheaval in their lives is emotionally traumatic for them.

Other Custody Issues: What Happens to the Divorcing Couple's Pets upon Divorce or Death?

For many people, pets are like family. The law says pets are property, although most pet owners tend to think of them more like children. When people get divorced, the legal question of what happens to the couple's pets poses an interesting combination of community property issues and custody arrangement issues.

I've had situations where we worked out a visitation plan for a divorcing couple's dog so that the dog's "daddy" would drop off the dog at doggie daycare and the dog's "mommy" would pick up the dog from doggie daycare. With this schedule, they traded off every other week to have custody of the dog, and they divided up the expenses of caring for the dog, including grooming and vet expenses. It was much like child custody and child support, but not enforceable by contempt.

Likewise, in estate planning, I have set up trusts to care for pets after their owners died. Many elderly people have a pet that has had constant attention from their owner, and those pets grieve when the owner dies. It is sad to think that not only will the pet lose their owner and their home, but they may end up in an animal shelter, and tragically it could be a kill shelter. Under the law, your pet is property, you cannot "leave property to your property" so you can't name your pet as a beneficiary in your Will as if the pet were a person. The pet has no ability to manage money on its own. However, in a trust, even a trust inside your Will, you can name a trustee to manage the property, and the trustee be charged with the duty to care for your pet.

While we tend to think of a pet in terms of a dog or cat, people often own pets such as birds that may live 80 years, or donkeys that may live 40 years, and those pets could very well out-live their owner. Besides, it may be much more difficult to find someone willing to take on the responsibility of a more unusual pet.

Of course, you could simply say in your will, "I give my dog to my daughter," if you trust that your daughter has the financial means, the skill, and the love necessary to care for your pet properly. But it may be that you would want to make a budget of how much you spend for food, vet care, dog walkers, toys, etc., and estimate how long the pet is expected to live, then set that money aside in a trust for the trustee (who could be your daughter) to make sure that your pet is well-cared for after you are gone.

Still Another Custody Issue: What Happens to Frozen Embryos upon Death or Divorce?

Still another type of "custody" issue that I've encountered is over the possession of frozen embryos.

While the debate rages on about when life begins and many people feel strongly that an embryo is a baby, the law is largely silent and still treats a frozen embryo-like property when it comes to the right of possession. However, there are people who offer their unused frozen embryos for adoption. Those are called "snowflake embryo adoptions," and there are adoption agencies for them. Whether the frozen embryo is a person or genetic material, the fate of the embryo should be addressed in advance for cases of divorce and death. Many people would be greatly distressed to simply have the frozen embryos destroyed.

I wrote one of the first legal treatises on assisted reproduction published back in 1986, entitled "A Time to be Born, A Time to Die, Alternative Reproduction and Texas Probate Law[1]." In that article, I mentioned a dilemma that has yet to be resolved: what is the legal result if an embryo is implanted years after the death of the father? That is entirely possible today. After all, the

---

[1] "A Time to be Born, A Time to Die: Alternative Reproduction and Texas Probate Law," by Laura D. Heard, 17 St. Mary's Law Journal 927 (1986).

heirs have been determined and property distributed in a decedent's estate, another biological child of the decedent could be born, possibly years later. The embryo was conceived during the marriage, although implanted much later, and the genetic DNA testing would prove the child to be that of the deceased. A child born after the execution of a Will, even if born after the person who made the Will has died, is normally entitled to a portion of the estate regardless of the fact that the child is not named in the Will. The law has not caught up with medical technology in this matter and while there are legal presumptions that a child born years later is not the child of the decedent, it could very well be proven that the child is, in fact, genetically the child of the decedent.

Likewise, in divorce situations, could child support be demanded for a child born of a frozen embryo much later after the divorce? Most frozen embryo banks try to address such contingencies by contract, but the legality of the contract might not stand up in court if challenged and some breaches of contract are not easily remedied. While the anonymous sperm donor is not liable for child support, the biological and intended father who was married to the mother and once consented to the procedure, is a different situation. The former husband might later be liable for child support even though consent for the procedure has impliedly been withdrawn because of the divorce. Certainly, there are many men who never intended to be fathers who are on the hook for child support. Texas law does not permit a pregnant woman to get divorced until after the baby is born, but with current medical technology, the woman might wait until well after the divorce is final and yet become pregnant with the former husband's child.

The best practice is to be specific and explicitly address in the divorce decree, as well as in the gestational agreement, these issues of future responsibility for child support of a child not yet in being or explicit instructions not to implant the embryo or to give it up for adoption.

Further, there is a monthly expense charged by the embryo bank to keep the embryo frozen. The payment of that monthly fee, the ownership/custody of the frozen embryo, and perhaps instructions to place the embryo for adoption should be specifically addressed in a divorce decree and in a Will. In divorce, one party should be awarded the possession of the embryo along with the responsibility to pay for the maintenance of the embryo, and in a Will, a person may want to assign some trust money for the future payment of those fees. As part of finalizing the divorce, one party may need to sign a power of attorney or voluntary relinquishment of parental rights to allow the other party to place the frozen embryo for adoption.

If a couple has created a frozen embryo together, this is not something their estate planning or divorce lawyer is likely to think about asking, and the client should be proactive to bring it up and make sure it is addressed. Who will have possession, what are the duties of the person in possession, and how will the expenses of maintaining the embryo or the expense of child support be paid? These are questions that should be addressed specifically in a divorce decree, the parents' Wills, and/or in a Living Trust. Failure to address the issue could lead to some expensive litigation or heartbreak later.

CHAPTER 4

HOW IS CHILD SUPPORT WORKED OUT UNDER TEXAS LAW?

When it comes to child support, the traditional arrangement has been that the children stay with the mother, and the father pays child support to her. However, this standard is changing as the circumstances of the world are changing. For instance, the traditional arrangement presupposes that the father makes more money than the mother. However, these days, there are many situations where the mother makes more money than the father.

Every child support arrangement and calculation is based on the dynamics of the family, the percentage of custody held by each parent, and the income of each parent. For example, let's say both parents have equal time with the children (as with a "one week on, one week off" schedule). If that is the case, the judge could calculate child support in several different ways. They may calculate how much the mother would owe the father for child support and vice versa (as if one or the other was the primary custodian), and then subtract one from the other, and whomever earns more money simply pays the difference or the offset amount. Or, in some cases, the Court can order payment of other things such as child care or extracurricular activities as child support, or waive child support altogether.

If both parents have approximately the same income and spend equal time with the children, child support is really up to the judge's discretion. There's a lot of discretion that a judge can utilize in family law, as far as the judge doing what he thinks is in the best interest of the children under the circumstances. For example, a Family Court judge can order more than standard child support or less than standard child support in any given case, depending on what they think the situation calls for, as long as the judge can articulate some evidence to support a good cause for the deviation.

Our rules on child support have not changed by much for many years. Just recently in 2021, though, a new child support schedule has been enacted that requires a lower percentage of income for the paying parent who has below a certain income. It is rumored that more expansive changes in the way we calculate child support may be coming in 2023. Beware if you rely on information from the internet to try to estimate what you will owe or receive in child support, because that information may soon be outdated.

Once child support has been ordered, it can only be changed by a new court order. Parties often make the mistake of thinking they can just have an agreement between themselves to reduce or eliminate child support, but they do not take into account that the Texas Attorney General is tracking the failure to pay child support. The Attorney General can suspend a person's driver's license or professional license for failure to pay child support, as well as take an income tax refund before it is distributed to someone who is behind on payments. Many a person was shocked to find that their personal stimulus payment(s) in 2020-21 were re-routed, without any prior notice, to their former spouse or lover to pay an old child support obligation. Many who received these child support payments were surprised too and had no idea it came from the other party's stimulus money. Child support enforcement may include jail time for failure to pay, and there are special courts dedicated to collecting child support that will not hesitate to use jail time as an incentive.

If you need to reduce or stop paying previously-ordered child support because of a change in circumstances, such as an injury that prevents you from working, it is important to see an attorney immediately to discuss how to get the process started for a new order to replace the old one. If you cannot afford an attorney, at least ask the Attorney General to review your current income and they can enter an order to reduce child support for the future.

Child Support delinquency does not disappear when a person dies, and there is a process for requesting the money from a decedent's estate. If the obligor dies before the child has reached age 18 and graduated from high school, future child support stops because there is no more income, but the prior debt for child support owed during life and not already paid remains. If the obligor dies while the children are still minors, then the surviving parent must usually look to other sources, such as life insurance, social security, or a trust for future child support, unless the decedent's estate is large enough to pay the child support. If you are in a situation where the person obligated to pay you child support has died while there is still a child support obligation, you should seek the advice of an attorney immediately to help you decide if you can make a claim against the estate in probate. If you are in the midst of divorce negotiations, you may want to seek an agreement to obligate the person paying child support to also maintain a life insurance policy for the benefit of the children. Again, you never know when death may occur.

When Alimony or Spousal Support is Awarded, How is the Amount Calculated?

First, we need to define our terminology in this discussion. Spousal "support" in Texas means support during the marriage. In temporary orders, particularly, the courts will quite often order one spouse to pay support to the other because as long as they are married, there is a legal duty to look out for the spouse's best interests, even though they are currently in an adversarial situation, at least to make sure the spouse has the basic necessities of life. When it comes to payments after divorce, what most people would call "alimony," Texas calls that "Spousal Maintenance." (Remember, "support" is during the marriage, "maintenance" is after marriage). I use the term "alimony" loosely here because that is what the non-lawyer would call it, although lawyers are quick to point out that we don't call it that in Texas.

Texas does permit alimony/spousal maintenance, but it is a relatively recent phenomenon. In fact, Texas was actually the last of the 50 states to allow alimony or spousal maintenance after divorce, only doing so around 25 years ago. When alimony/spousal maintenance was first introduced in Texas, it was only allowed in cases of domestic violence and only lasted two years after the divorce.

Now, according to the statute, it is possible to get spousal maintenance for life, but in only extremely limited cases of inability to work, and other than that, the maximum period of time for it to last is 10 years (and only if the couple has been married at least 30 years at the time of divorce). These days, Texas judges take a number of factors into consideration when deciding if spousal maintenance should be granted, but all of them place limits on how much and how long it can be granted, such as:

- The length of time that the couple has been married (as alimony is only granted when a couple has been married for an extended period of time, usually at least 10 years of marriage)
- Whether the spouse is disabled and/or capable of working

- Whether there is a disabled child that the spouse is going to have to care for in perpetuity
- Whether there was a history of domestic violence in the marriage.

Spousal maintenance is only assigned and calculated based on the reasonable needs of the less financially stable recipient-spouse. There is no automatic standard percentage as in child support. You have to show evidence of what that receiving spouse's income is or should be, and how much they would need to accommodate a budget to meet their minimum reasonable needs (with reasonableness being determined by the judge). But the judge will also consider the needs of the paying spouse's budget as well.

The hesitance of judges to grant spousal maintenance is reflected in how many rules and limitations there are to it if it is granted, such as:

- **Budget Veto Powers:** The judge has the discretion to slash any budget proposed by a spousal maintenance recipient, cutting it down to whatever that judge thinks is reasonable to barely meet the person's actual needs.

- **20% of Income Cap:** Spousal maintenance cannot be more than 20% of the paying spouse's gross income. Notably, 20% is the limit, not the norm. The cap doesn't mean that you automatically get 20% of the paying spouse's income. Rather, it simply means that you can't get more than 20% of the paying spouse's income, after you prove what you really need.
- **No Increases nor Requests for New Maintenance After the Divorce:** Alimony/spousal maintenance, if awarded at all, must be ordered at the time of divorce. You can't come and ask for spousal maintenance after the divorce is finalized. Additionally, once the divorce is granted, alimony/spousal maintenance payments can never be increased to more than what was ordered during the divorce process. However, the paying spouse can request that it be lowered or stopped for a change in circumstances.

- **Hard Stops to Support:** Alimony/spousal maintenance stops automatically if either party dies, or if the party receiving support gets remarried or even lives with another person in a sexual relationship. This is fairly standard in most states.

Generally, spousal maintenance is only ordered for a certain number of years (based on how long you have been married). Usually, the judges order even fewer years than the law allows. The only cases where Texas judges may grant lifetime support are cases where the receiving spouse is disabled or has to care for a disabled child.

The thinking behind the limited nature of alimony/spousal maintenance and the hesitance to grant it in Texas is that Texas is a community property state. This means that all property and assets that were obtained during the marriage (with some exceptions) are community property and subject to division in any manner the judge thinks is fair. After divorce, there is no further duty towards the former spouse even if the former spouse meets with some tragedy or becomes unable to work after divorce. At the time of divorce, a judge can divide the community property in a way that is more favorable to the spouse who needs it more instead of awarding alimony/spousal maintenance. Judges would rather give you more than half of the community property than give you spousal maintenance after a divorce.

As such, alimony/spousal maintenance usually has the further qualifier of only really being assigned in cases where there is no property (or not enough property) to be divided, and/or in cases where there are more debts than property. Often, alimony/spousal maintenance assigned in these cases will only last for 2-5 years after the divorce, to allow the receiving party to get back on their feet. Even if the statute allows for five or seven years of maintenance, the judge may decide to only award one or two years. This is usually enough time to go to school and get the beginnings of a career established, but the requesting party must convince the judge that they are serious about school or have already started a program. Often, spousal maintenance of that sort is assigned if the receiving party is a former stay-at- home-mom who hasn't worked in many years *and* if there isn't enough community property and she has no other source of income. It is intended to help with the transition period, while the spouse who is re-entering the workforce tries to figure out what they're going to do for income for the rest of their life.

While alimony or spousal maintenance may be more difficult to get in Texas than in other states, it is not impossible. It is very much up to two factors:

- The facts of the case (and if the case qualifies for spousal maintenance by Texas standards)
- Whether the proposed recipient's attorney can be persuasive enough about granting support to their client.

At one time, the advantage of paying alimony/spousal maintenance was that the paying spouse could claim it as an income tax deduction while the receiving spouse had to claim it as income. This is no longer true under current federal income tax law.

Since it no longer counts as a deduction, some people have lost the financial incentive to pay alimony, but the law might change again in the future. Those who settled a divorce in the past by agreeing to pay alimony because it was a tax deduction have now lost that benefit but are still obligated to pay.

When federal tax law provided that alimony deduction, it was necessary to distinguish between a property division payment and alimony in order to claim it as a deduction. It will still make a difference to the one receiving the payments as to whether they have to count it as income for income tax. If, for example, you were to receive a portion of your former spouse's retirement income because it was earned during the marriage, that is not alimony, but instead, it is a division of community property earned during the marriage. A property division might not be counted as income. There are sometimes other streams of money coming after divorce, such as one spouse paying out the equity in the house to the other over time or reimbursing the other spouse for some debt, which are also property divisions, not alimony. There have been many disputes over whether certain payments after divorce are alimony or property division.

This distinction between alimony and property division could also make a difference in cases of the former spouse filing for bankruptcy. While child support and alimony are not discharged in bankruptcy, other obligations might be. These are all considerations that must be weighed when deciding how to divide property in a settlement agreement, and before making a final decision to agree, one should consult with tax and financial experts.

One other feature of alimony is that it usually ends upon the death of either party. Thus, a property division claim might be made against the decedent's estate, but alimony would have ceased at the death of the one paying. In the reverse situation, if the one receiving payments dies, the alimony obligation stops, but if it is a property division, the estate executor can still collect the property payments for the estate beneficiaries.

SECTION II
ESTATE PLANNING

CHAPTER 5

IMPACT OF DIVORCE ON ESTATE PLANNING DOCUMENTS

Oftentimes, when married couples sit down to write out their wills, they say, "I leave everything to my spouse, and if my spouse predeceases me, then everything equally to my children." This works fine in many cases.

However, if a married couple is going through a divorce, each party is advised to change their respective wills as soon as possible to reflect that changed relationship. In most divorce cases, neither party wants their half of the community property to go to their soon-to-be-ex-spouse, particularly if that spouse was abusive or broke up the marriage with an affair, an addiction, or terrible spending habits.

There have been several times in my career where death became an issue in the middle of a divorce; where I was in the middle of handling a couple's divorce when one of the parties unexpectedly died or was murdered. In those cases, the issue of divorce immediately went away. You can't divorce a dead person. If you're in the process of a divorce and the other party passes away before the divorce is finalized, then they died while married to you. Life goes on and the estate is processed as if the divorce lawsuit never happened, or there was never a divorce pending. That often doesn't make sense to the surviving parents or children of the deceased who were aware of the pending divorce. Those surviving family members do not see the surviving spouse as deserving of the estate earned by the estranged spouse, but the law doesn't care, except in cases of the murder of one spouse by the other. One cannot inherit from a spouse or collect their life insurance after murdering them. Lots of relatives feel like if a divorce was pending at the time of death, it should be treated like a murder, but that simply is not the case.

To prevent the outcome of leaving one's estate to an estranged spouse, I always suggest that my clients change their wills right at the beginning of the divorce process. This way, if something happens to them before the process is finalized, their actual wishes will be carried out at least as far as their separate property and half of the community property. In a community property state, you can only give half of the community property to a non-spouse during the marriage, but at least that is better than giving all of it to the estranged spouse.

I've had several cases where the husband stated in his Will that the marital home he occupied with his second wife, was to go to his adult children of his first marriage. This presents a problem to the surviving widow when the adult children want to throw her out and sell the house. If the house is community property, the widow owns half the house regardless of the will, since the husband can only give away his half. Where multiple owners of a house cannot agree on whether to sell it, normally they can get a court order for the sale in what is called a "partition" suit.

However, the Texas Estates code and our homestead laws protect the widow for her lifetime if she chooses to live there. I've been able to assure the widow that a surviving spouse or minor children who occupy the homestead, cannot be evicted or have their home sold out from under them as long as they continue to live there, even if the house was the husband's sole and separate property. The widow may live there for the rest of her life, but if she dies or moves out, then it is fair game and the house may be sold and the money divided, even without her consent.

The same is not true if an unmarried couple occupy a house together. The surviving girlfriend or boyfriend who is not gifted the house in the Will and has no ownership of the house, has no right to continue living there after the owner of the house dies.

Timing is everything in these situations and you have no control, usually, over the time of your death. In one case that I handled, the parties had reached a written agreement in mediation, but had not yet gone before a judge to finalize the divorce, when one spouse died. In that case, the divorce was dismissed due to the death and the mediation agreement became void. Because the death occurred before divorce, the surviving spouse would have had a homestead interest regardless of the deceased spouse's Will and regardless of the agreement for who would get the property at divorce. A deceased person cannot get divorced, and the parties were still married when he died.

In another similar case, the parties had orally proved the agreed divorce in court and the judge had verbally declared them divorced, but the written final decree had not yet been signed by the Judge when one spouse died. In that case, the divorce went forward after the death because the parties were already legally divorced, and the written order was just a formality memorializing what had already occurred in court. In that case, if divorce had already awarded the house to the husband, then because the death occurred after the divorce, even if less than 24 hours after the divorce was orally pronounced, then the house belonged to ex-husband who was awarded it in the divorce, and ex-wife would have no homestead protection because she was no longer married to the decedent at the moment of his death.

Even if the deceased ex-husband never changed his old Will that left the house to his wife (now ex-wife), the law presumes that he did not want his ex-spouse to get his property. This presumption of law appears for Wills, Trusts, and Life Insurance policies. However, this doesn't change the fact that if you haven't changed your will to reflect your post-divorce wishes, you should do so as soon as possible. Beyond needing to change your ex-spouse's position as your main beneficiary, there are other issues raised by the divorce that you will likely want to consider.

For instance, if your will names your ex-spouse's relatives as successors, executors, trustees, or guardians for your children. These appointments might have been easy, logical choices when you initially signed off on the will as a joint decision with your then-spouse. However, after the divorce, your relationships with your ex-spouse's relatives may have changed, and you may not want them in the same positions when it comes to your estate (as well as potential guardianship over your children).

If you do decide to remove ex-in-laws, or soon-to-be ex-in-laws, from any position in your will (whether as successor, heir, trustee, executor, guardian, or anything else), you should think carefully about whom you would like instead as a substitute to replace them, and potentially have the requisite conversations with the new appointees. In any case, it's a good idea to re-evaluate your will in light of a divorce and make any necessary changes right away. You do not ever have to keep a will that is the mirror image of your spouse's will, even if you are not getting divorced.

If you have a living trust jointly with an estranged spouse, you should discuss with your lawyer when and how to revoke it or whether you want to keep it. That may depend on the terms written in the trust document, and the property division in the divorce. Make sure that your attorney knows that the property is owned by the trust, not by you and your spouse, when making your inventory for the divorce.

And speaking of what happens to your minor children after you die, I have seen many single parents worry about that very issue. The law presumes that the other parent should have full custody, even though that other parent may have had little to no contact with the children up until that time. If the single parent is a widow, and the children are now true orphans, the relatives of the deceased husband might seek custody and have priority over a stepparent who actually raised the children. The paternal grandparents, for example, could legally step into the shoes of their deceased son who was the father. There are a couple of pre-planning options to consider protecting the rights of the surviving stepparent, but without planning ahead, the stepparent has a difficult task to try to overcome a blood relative's right to the children. The parent who feels strongly that the ex-spouse is not a good parent, should name someone as guardian for the children in their will, and even consider filing suit to make the stepparent a joint managing conservator if the other parent is deceased. It may be easier to add a joint-managing conservator while you, the parent, are alive, rather than after your death when the children come with money from your estate attached.

It is important to take a look at your will and make necessary changes even if you remain close with your ex-spouse and their family members and want to keep them in their respective positions in your will.

I have had a few clients who actually did want their ex-spouse to be the executor of their estate and serve as the guardian for their children after a divorce. However, even in that situation, it is necessary to make changes to your will after divorce. In fact, the best way to ensure that your ex-spouse remains the executor of your estate and the trustee for your minor children's inheritance is to make an entirely new will after your divorce, even if it says more or less the same thing as your pre-divorce will. This is because, as mentioned above, the law presumes that you don't want your ex-spouse to inherit your assets or be the executor of your estate. If the Court sees a will that pre-dates your divorce giving everything to your now-ex-spouse, the law dictates that the judge treats your ex-spouse as dead and makes a legal assumption that you simply forgot to change your will. This is true no matter how many people testify that you still wanted your ex-spouse to be in charge. The ex-spouse cannot inherit your property nor be the executor of your Will unless you make a new Will after the date of divorce.

When it comes to wills, people need to be aware that nothing happens automatically. Many people assume that if they die, their house will just automatically go to their spouse whether or not there is a Will, or they assume that if there is a Will, the house automatically belongs to them. However, it doesn't work like that in Texas. If you don't have a will saying that your spouse gets your property, you will encounter difficulty at the very least. The process of changing the title on a house after the owner has died is expensive and time-consuming, and not guaranteed to work if there is no probate of a valid Will. Even if the end result is that your spouse gets the property, it is not an automatic or easy process without a Will. If you have a Will, it still must go through probate first before it is any good.

I have often seen cases where dad dies, and mom continues to live in the house. She has every right to live there, but what she doesn't realize is that she cannot sell or transfer ownership of the entire house because it was community property, and she is not the sole owner even though her spouse has died. As long as someone pays the mortgage and the property taxes, no one will challenge mom's right to live there, but if a fire or some other damage occurs to the house and a claim is made to the homeowner's insurance, the insurance company will most likely issue a check that only the deceased person or his Executor can cash. Perhaps the insurance might make an electronic payment directly to a bank account that was joint between husband and wife, but once mom passes away, the children will definitely not be able to collect on the homeowner's insurance or sell the house that is titled in the deceased parents' names. At that point, a probate court must be involved. The longer you wait after the death of the first owner, the more difficult it gets to transfer the title.

Many times, nothing happens during mom's lifetime, but then when she passes away, her children cannot sell the house without probating both estates of mom and dad. If an adult child continues to live in the house without doing anything about probate, then by the time that adult child dies, it is even more of a mess because now you must probate three decedent's estates, and so much time has passed that it may be too late to probate some of them. The probate of an estate must occur within four years of the date of death. The person living in the house may feel that because he paid the taxes and lived there exclusively, he has an exclusive right to the house, when, in fact, there may be many other descendants of the deceased parents who have an equal right to the house. Add to the legal nightmare a relative who is a minor child or a person who lacks the mental capacity to consent to anything, and you have a situation that is nearly impossible to fix. Not only would it be difficult to sell that house, but also, because none of the original owners of the house have survived, the mortgage company may refuse to give any information to the persons who are actually paying the mortgage, and they cannot take out a home equity loan or refinance because they don't legally own the house.

There are some things we can do to try to work around the situation just described, but no matter what we do at that point, the house will forever have what we call "a cloud on the title," meaning that there is a legal problem with the ownership and the buyer takes a risk when buying it that someone else could sue later claiming that they own at least part of it. The value of the house is diminished, and it may be more difficult to find a buyer. In some instances, financial institutions will refuse to loan money for a mortgage so the only way to sell it is for cash or owner financing. Situations like this are easily avoided if a valid Will is probated in time.

Even when the surviving spouse remains in the house, there are many factors to consider, such as whether the house was bought during the marriage or before the marriage, which affects whether the decedent's children or other relatives have any claim to the house.

In cases where the house is truly the only asset, we can even do what is known as a "transfer on death deed," during the owner's lifetime. There are some pros and cons to deeding the house to your beneficiaries before death, but it is an option to consider, and it is definitely better than no plan at all. If you are considering just deeding your house to your adult children before you die, you should carefully inquire about the effect on your property tax exemptions for homestead and over 65, and the effect on the recipient's income tax, future capital gains tax, as well as the possibility of a gift tax. Otherwise, after recording the deed, you may find a very unpleasant spike in your property taxes, income tax, or find that you cannot get a home improvement loan that you need unless your children deed the house back to you. And there might be no recourse if the recipient refuses to deed it back to you in some instances. There is a possible revocable deed, but it would have to be set up that way from the beginning.

Do Most People Know That They Need to Put New Estate Planning Documents in Place After a Texas Divorce?

There are a few things that people generally do not understand when it comes to this subject. One is the fact that a will has no intrinsic value in Texas if it doesn't go through probate. Another is that even though you think the meaning of the Will is clear, it might not be legally valid.

Most people believe that judges in Probate Court can simply do what they think is right, or that if a judge knows what you would have wanted, then they can just make that happen. In many areas of

Texas law, such as divorce or contract law, this is absolutely a fair assumption. One good example can be found in divorce matters, where judges have more discretion with their rulings to do what they think is right within the bounds of the law. For instance, when a judge divides property in a Texas divorce case, they don't have to divide it equally between spouses. Rather, if they think one party or the other deserves a larger share, they can rule accordingly. The law calls that a "just and right division" of property. Although most of the time the judges try to make the division more or less 50/50, they often make adjustments and the way they divide it cannot be challenged just because it is not 50/50.

Another good example is contract law. Texas judges overseeing contract law cases will almost always focus on questions of intent if the written words are not clear. They examine what the intention was behind the writing, signing, or violation of the terms of a contract, and often rule accordingly. They can set aside a contract that is grossly unfair.

However, the laws governing wills and probate are extremely strict and give the presiding judges little room for discretion. Fairness has nothing to do with it. The premise is that once you die, you can't own property and the government has the right to decide what happens to your property. Unless you follow the instructions given by the government in the statutes exactly, you have no right to direct what happens to your property. Probate judges are compelled to do exactly what the law says, even when they know that it's obviously not in line with what the deceased person would have wanted. Wills must not only have the correct wording but they must be signed by witnesses and the testator in the right order. People don't usually realize how tightly probate judges are bound by the exact letter of the law, even and sometimes especially, in situations where it's directly contrary to the decedent's actual wishes or is otherwise unfair.

In one particular case, the deceased person, let's call him "Tim," left an unsigned Will and had named a friend, let's call him "Bob," as the Executor. Tim also named Bob as his agent in a valid Power of Attorney. However, all powers of attorney are immediately void as soon as the person who made it dies, and an unsigned

Will has absolutely no effect. Tim also left a note saying what he wanted done with his house, but his note didn't qualify as a Will. Tim verbally told many people that he wanted Bob to have the house once Tim was gone. None of that mattered. Although there was plenty of evidence, testimonial and written, that Tim wanted Bob to get all his property and be in charge of the estate, with no contest and no evidence to the contrary, still there was no valid Will, so the property passed under the law to other relatives who never even knew Tim. The judge had no choice. A simple Will would have made a huge difference for Bob.

CHAPTER 6

ESTATE PLANNING DOCUMENTS MARRIED COUPLES SHOULD HAVE IN PLACE

For estate planning, couples and individuals alike always need to leave **wills,** whether or not they have a trust. In addition, if their estate is large enough that they might have to pay estate tax, then they need to take steps to avoid that tax. The estate tax can be brutal: in some cases, paying the tax can mean losing more than half of your estate to the government.

As of 2022, if you have an estate that is worth less than $12.06 million, then you don't have to worry about a federal estate tax. But in 2026, the IRS plans to lower that value to $5 million, adjusted for inflation. Therefore, as a general rule of thumb, when people ask about estate tax, I ask them whether they have close to $5 million in their total estate or expect to by the time they die. If you are not even near $5 million in your total estate, then you really don't have to worry about estate tax in Texas, unless you win big in the lottery or unless there is another change in the law. This is because Texas mirrors the federal estate tax exclusion amounts, which is not true in all states. Stay tuned. It is a good idea to at least check in with your CPA, financial planner, or attorney every few years to make sure that neither the federal nor the state law has changed to your detriment on estate tax.

There are a few methods to avoid estate tax, including getting your estate below the value where the federal estate tax kicks in, as long as your property is in Texas. Currently, you can give away $16,000 per person per year to as many people as you wish in order to reduce the value of your estate during your lifetime. For an older couple who are just barely over the exclusion limit, giving enough away in annual gifts may be all they need to do to avoid estate tax. This federal gift tax limit changes fairly regularly. It is important to stay tuned to such changes as they can make a drastic difference in the type of estate planning that you need.

The other, more efficient way to completely avoid the estate tax is with something like a **living trust** or an **LLC**. A living trust is one you set up and fund during your lifetime, naming a trustee to manage the trust estate. Sometimes, a similar trust in a Will, called a "testamentary trust," can accomplish the same goal. Whether a living trust or a testamentary trust, the trustee must manage the property for the benefit of the beneficiaries. You can be your own trustee and your own beneficiary, as long as you name a successor trustee and beneficiary to take over after you die.

Alternatively, a person might avoid estate tax using an LLC, (Limited Liability Company), which is often used for business. Some of the members of the LLC, similar to stockholders, get to vote on how the LLC is managed, but there are voting and nonvoting members. The concepts sound simple, but the documents forming these entities as well as the income tax ramifications can be quite confusing and complicated. However, for a family-owned business, farm, ranch or real estate holdings, the LLC may make sense for management purposes as well as estate tax purposes. If the property belongs to the LLC rather than the individual person, then it is not in the individual's estate for tax purposes.

Generally, very wealthy people usually have their estates set up in such a way that they don't ever have to worry about the estate tax. It's the people whose estates are just over the limit that get stuck paying the estate tax, almost always because they didn't know to plan ahead. It is a kind of upper-middle-class tragedy. Oftentimes, it's the family farm or ranch that ends up being sacrificed and sold to pay the estate tax, because that land is worth enough money that the estate tax kicks in. Especially in Texas, there are family farms and ranches that have belonged to the same family for generations. Families like that often never really had enough money to think that they were wealthy, certainly not to the extent that they would have to take measures to avoid the estate tax. But the land has risen in value over the years and when the family patriarch and matriarch pass away, all of a sudden, they owe tax perhaps in the amount of 55% of the value of the land. Then tragically, they must sell the land to pay the tax because they can't raise the money any other way. This may be where the common saying comes from that if you don't have a Will, the State gets all your property when you die. The irony is that, in this example, a trust, not a Will, would be what is needed. For those families, a living trust would have literally saved the family farm.

Another example of the government getting the property of a person who died without a Will is when the estate is too small to justify the expense of going through the process of proving the heirs without a Will. Although a relative might be entitled under the law to get the meager bank account of the decedent, the cost of probate without a Will is so much more than the procedure with a good Will, that it makes no sense to pay the fees in order to get the account, and therefore, the money is eventually sent to the State Comptroller as abandoned property. Finally, there are people with no living relatives to make a claim, and in those cases, too, the property goes to the State unless they have a Will.

I like to discuss living trusts in these conversations because they can be a remarkably effective tool for avoiding estate tax but are often assigned a wider utility than is realistic in Texas. People are so concerned about avoiding estate tax, but they never realize that their estate is not large enough to ever owe estate tax. There are several situations where a living trust is a really good idea, but most people do not have to worry about estate tax in Texas, and most people here don't actually need a living trust. This is contrary to what people often hear about living trusts: often people hear that everyone needs to avoid probate, which is not necessarily true in Texas. Many people think that they need a living trust when they don't, while many people who really do need a living trust often do not realize that they do or they just keep procrastinating until it is too late.

This trust situation has something to do with how probate works in Texas. Our state has a fairly streamlined probate process as long as you have a good Will, and it is much less of a hassle to put a will through probate here than it is to do so in most other states. In states where probate should be avoided at all costs because it is a complicated, expensive nightmare, utilizing a living trust and managing that trust to avoid probate may make a lot of sense. On the other hand, putting a will through the streamlined probate process in Texas is actually much less of a hassle for the average estate than managing a living trust and the expense may be about the same either way. Living trusts are expensive to create and often don't accomplish the goal of avoiding probate. The trust document is usually very long, full of legal language, and very intimidating.

In contrast, if a person owns property in California, for example, at this time, California has a state-imposed estate tax which is far below the federal exclusion threshold and far below the value of any real estate there, so any person who owns even a modest house in California may need a living trust there to avoid estate tax. So if you live in Texas but own real estate in other states, then a living trust may make sense. Also, every state has its own probate laws, so if you own land or mineral interests in multiple states, the easiest way to pass that to the next generation may be through a trust.

People also often want to use a trust to avoid paying damages to creditors or because they fear losing a lawsuit or to get their estate below the threshold to qualify for government assistance. These reasons should be discussed carefully with an attorney because many times it simply will not work. As long as the trust is "revocable" there are instances where the court will order it revoked, and if there are known creditors or lawsuits pending at the time of trust creation, the trust will be void.

There is a trust, called a "supplemental income trust" that can be used to avoid losing government assistance, but it is only applicable to certain situations where the monthly income is the only thing disqualifying the recipient from benefits.

Although the most common trust is a "revocable living trust," sometimes a non-revocable trust is required in order to accomplish the goal. Early in my career, I represented a famous movie star/Hollywood producer who had been named Executor of his elderly aunt's Will in Corpus Christi. The Aunt had set up a trust during her lifetime to benefit a niece whom she later wanted to disinherit due to some squabble. She instructed the Executor of her Will to revoke the non-revocable Trust and use the cash to pay the taxes. He tried unsuccessfully to do that, and he spent several years and all the estate cash in unsuccessful litigation before the IRS came calling. In the meantime, he had delivered to several museums some fine art pieces for safekeeping, which he later needed to sell so the estate could pay taxes because he could not revoke the trust and the estate had no more cash. The donations of art were charitable donations made to avoid taxes, but there were taxes, nevertheless, and the estate had no liquid assets. You see, if the estate doesn't have enough money to pay the estate debts, then at least some of the beneficiaries lose what they were supposed to get under the Will. Everywhere the executor turned, the recipients of the estate assets were angry as he tried to take away what he had already given them, but he needed to satisfy the federal government. That's when he hired me to retrieve some of the art he had sent to museums. If only the Decedent had been advised as to the impossibility of revoking the trust and the tax consequences of those actions, she would have saved her executor many sleepless nights or if the Executor had realized that the Will was requiring an impossible task, he might have saved himself years of stress.

While it is easy for a person to change his or her Will during their lifetime, it is not so easy to change a deed and sometimes it is not easy to change a living trust or the terms of a corporate entity.

There are a lot of estate planning "professionals," many of them non-lawyers and many not even from Texas, who try to scare laypeople into thinking they need to avoid probate just like they need to avoid the estate tax. If they tell you that you need to avoid Texas probate at all costs, and the only way to do that is through a living trust, then all they're really doing is selling living trusts. I get upset any time I hear a speaker talking to a large crowd and telling everyone that they need a living trust when the speaker has no idea what the financial situation of all those people maybe. It may be that not one person in the audience has an estate large enough to incur any estate tax. There is not one blanket, one-trust-works-for-everyone solution. The decision on whether or not to make a living trust is very much dependent on the individual's total situation.

The truth is that many times the living trust does not even truly avoid probate altogether. Everyone who creates a living trust will make a Will to go along with it that says any property that they forgot to put in the trust will go into the trust after they die. People are not perfect, and they often forget to include one or another thing that they own when putting together a living trust or they assume that the person who set up the living trust took care of all of that. Trusts have to be managed, not just thrown in a drawer and forgotten like a Will. When the Maker passes away, if they didn't include everything they own in the trust by transferring title to the trust properly, all the remaining property in the individual's name must then go into the trust and the only way to do that is to probate the will in addition to having a living trust. I know of one man who thought he had put all his property into a trust or given it away before death, but right before he died, a life insurance policy or investment declared a dividend and issued stock in his individual name. The family had to probate his Will solely because of that stock certificate.

In Texas, setting up and maintaining a living trust can be surprisingly more expensive than probate would have been, and a lot more complicated. Often, people end up paying money for a living trust and then ultimately dissolving it for various reasons. People don't like having a notebook full of documents that they don't understand and wondering whether they are supposed to be doing more to manage their trust than they are aware of. The trust document is long and difficult to read, causing fear that they may violate the terms because they don't understand them.

One of the most common reasons for dissolving a living trust is that in certain cases, the trust can prevent the person from getting a home equity loan since their only asset is the house and it's contained in the living trust. They paid money to deed their house into the trust, and now they must pay money to get the house out of the trust so that they can get a loan. Also, if the trust is revocable, as most living trusts are, it might not help at all to protect assets from some creditors or from the government when applying for Medicaid. When a person realizes that they have a legal document that they don't understand, they often regret making the trust.

When helping people who are trying to figure out if they need a living trust, I always ask if the following situations apply to them:

- Do you have an estate tax issue, or is it highly unlikely that you would ever be charged an estate tax?
- Do you have a property in multiple states?
- Do you have real estate, oil, or gas interests in other states besides Texas?
- Are you planning on doing something that's likely to cause a will contest, like disinheriting one of your children?
- Does Alzheimer's run in your family or do you have cause to fear that you might be mentally unable to manage your own finances in the future?

If they say yes, then I tell them that a living trust may be particularly useful for them, depending on the specifics of their situation. If they say no, then it is more likely than not that they, like most people in Texas, do not need a living trust. However, whether or not they have a living trust, everyone needs a Will.

Life Insurance

Another thing to consider when looking at estate planning is life insurance. Life insurance payments to beneficiaries pass outside of your estate. That is, they go directly to whoever is named as the beneficiary of the policy. While your will may say, "I leave everything equally to my five children," that will not apply to any life insurance policy unless you explicitly name all of your children as beneficiaries on the policy itself. If you make one child the beneficiary of your insurance policy, you may have highly favored that child without realizing it, since the life insurance payout will go to them and them alone. For this reason, it's essential to look at your life insurance policies and beneficiaries when doing your estate planning. In order to change beneficiaries, you must get a form and give written instructions to the life insurance company. You can't do that in your Will.

By the way, if your children are minors when you die, the insurance company will not pay them directly and the company won't automatically pay the surviving parent on the children's behalf. The insurance company will require the surviving parent to go to probate court and be appointed guardian of the children, which requires them to put up a bond. Therefore, it is wise to name a trustee as the beneficiary of the life insurance on behalf of the minor children. You will need to direct the trustee on the terms of when to distribute the money to the children, and you will have to request a form from the insurance company to change your beneficiary if you already have the children listed as individual beneficiaries. The forms don't usually give you much room to write, but you might try to name the beneficiary as "My child, Mary, provided she has reached the age of 25, or if she is younger, then to Tom my trustee for the benefit of my child, Mary."

Life insurance can be used for many things such as to pay for a burial, to fund a trust after you die, to pay estate taxes, to make a final gift to a favorite charity, or to keep a business enterprise going after you die. Anyone who runs a small business should consider having a life insurance policy with a named Trustee to manage payroll for at least a few key employees in case of the unexpected death of the owner. There are also life insurance policies that can be used in case of disability as a form of long-term care insurance for the insured.

Powers of Attorney

I always recommend that when people are putting their wills together, they should also go ahead and do their powers of attorney at the same time. Just as a will is only good after you have died, conversely powers of attorney are only good while you are still alive. They exist to ensure that you are cared for if you become incapacitated. That is, if you are in a coma, under heavy sedation, unconscious, have dementia, or otherwise incapacitated to the point where you cannot manage your own affairs, a power of attorney allows an agent or proxy to step in and handle your affairs for you.

There are two kinds of powers of attorney, which are notably separate and cannot be combined into one document:

1. Medical Power of Attorney (for healthcare decisions)
2. Statutory Financial Powers of Attorney (for real estate and financial decisions)

A **Medical Power of Attorney** gives your agent the right to make any kind of health care decision that you could make, including putting you in a nursing home or disconnecting artificial life support. You can choose to keep it extremely broad or limit which powers you choose to give your agent. It is important to make sure your agent knows your desires on medical treatment since they are supposed to carry out your wishes even if they disagree with your choices. While the Medical Power of Attorney gives an agent decision-making power, a simple **HIPAA release** would allow as many people as you choose to have the ability to know your medical condition and treatment options without giving them the right to make any decisions.

A **Statutory Financial Power of Attorney**, on the other hand, allows your agent to make any decisions about your property, finances, and assets that you could make, including paying your bills, managing your investments, selling your real estate, and handling your bank accounts. These can be tailored and limited in scope or be very broad. For example, if you were to be overseas for work or military service and need to sell some real estate, you might give someone a power of attorney that is limited to permitting your agent only to sell a particular piece of land and it could have an expiration date after which the power of attorney is no longer effective.

Since many of these documents require the signatures of two witnesses and a notary, I recommend to that people knock them out all in one sitting. During the estate planning session where you are signing or finalizing your will, you could also sign a medical power of attorney and a statutory power of attorney, as well as some other related documents.

While the two witnesses and a notary are handy, many people also decide to sign a document called a **Directive to Physicians**. This document speaks to your future doctor directly and expresses your wishes regarding artificial life support. You can use a Directive to Physicians to tell the doctor that you don't want life support under any circumstances, that you do want life support but only in specific circumstances, or that you always want life support no matter what. The Directive to Physicians is what is commonly referred to as a **"Living Will,"** not to be confused with a Will or with a Living Trust. The Medical Power of Attorney may give an agent the right to decide whether or not to terminate life support, or it may simply state that there is a Directive to Physicians which you expect your agent to honor and enforce.

These documents can get rather specific. Life support is more complicated than it appears in the popular imagination, and life support decisions are not just a matter of "pulling the plug" or not. Rather, you can specify your wishes for all kinds of things. For example, many directives to physicians include specifications about "artificially administered nutrition and hydration" (i.e., artificially prolonging someone's life by inserting feeding tubes into their gastrointestinal tract for food, and IVs into their veins for liquid hydration). Some people feel strongly that they would want one but not the other. One should also consider whether to administer defibrillation, dialysis, and CPR as life support measures. It is a good idea to consult with a physician or nurse to discuss the possibilities.

Along those lines, there is also the option of a DNR ("do not resuscitate") order for emergencies. The **out-of-hospital DNR** is used by hospice so that EMTs won't administer life-saving measures before transporting to a hospital where a doctor would be bound by the Directive to Physicians.

Putting these documents in place requires a significant degree of thought on several important questions. It requires you to really think through the different kinds of life support, and whether you would want each one in a variety of different situations, and if so, for how long.

Cremation

When making specifications about what happens to you as you pass away and after you die, you should also consider the issue of **cremation** (if applicable). Lots of people these days want to be cremated. In fact, more people are cremated than buried these days, primarily because it is a less expensive route. However, Texas law operates on the presumption that people do not want to be cremated, or at least, there seem to be more hurdles to get it done unless everyone agrees.

This can cause major issues for people who want to be cremated, and specifically for their families as they try to carry out their loved one's wishes. Since burial in the ground is considered the default, anyone can be buried that way without any advance planning. However, if you want to be cremated and don't plan ahead, the person left in charge may have to get permission from the majority of your adult children, and/or have something in writing from the deceased person that specifies that they wanted to be cremated. If anyone objects to the cremation before it occurs, generally a court order is going to be required and that takes time.

I have seen situations where adult children refuse to agree to cremation despite the clear wishes of the decedent. I have seen fights erupt between children about whether or not to cremate their parent's body, which can last for some time. Meanwhile, the funeral home charges a fee to store the body until the family can decide what to do with it. I have had to set a hearing and get court orders on whether a person can be cremated or not. A little advance planning on the part of the deceased person could have avoided all that litigation.

If you want to be cremated, the best way to avoid this type of contention is to sign a document called a **Designation of Agent to Control Remains**. This document designates someone to take charge of your remains (body/ashes) once you pass away. It puts that agent in charge of handling your funeral and getting your body buried or cremated, whichever you prefer, and where to place your ashes.

By the way, because of the increased popularity of cremation, many families have decided not to use a burial plot that was previously purchased. Burial plots have value, although it is not easy to re-sell one particularly since more people are choosing not to use one. There are brokers who help sell them and the plot can be appraised. Burial plots are often overlooked as real estate owned by a decedent on the inventories for both probate cases and in case of divorce.

Most likely, a divorcing couple will no longer want to be buried next to one another, so one or the other will need to take the entire plot in the property division or it will have to be sold. It is another item that is often overlooked at the time of divorce and which can cause contention years later, even into the next generation.

When finalizing your will and your powers of attorney, another thing to be careful and deliberate about is the question of **guardianship**. This could mean guardianship for you, in case you ever require one, and/or guardianship of any children you may have, in case they ever require one. Generally, guardianship for yourself is the last resort, and one hopefully avoided by a good set of medical and statutory powers of attorney, but if one becomes absolutely necessary, you can designate ahead of time who you would want that to be. I'll talk more about guardianships later in this book.

Of course, as I have previously discussed, naming a guardian for your minor children in case you die is one of the central parts of any parent's will. However, it helps to go a step further. It takes at least a couple of weeks to get through the probate process. What if you were in a car accident with your children, you were all medically incapacitated, and somebody needed to make immediate decisions about your children's health care?

To preemptively address that scenario, you can put a **medical power of attorney** in place for your minor children. This document will allow you to name a person or several people (as well as alternates in case your primary choice is not available) who could be an agent for you to make health care decisions for your children as needed until they reach age 18. This would give them the immediate ability to step in and make those decisions without having to wait for a parent's will to be probated or a guardian to be appointed for your children. A medical power of attorney for one's minor children is a good idea for a single parent whenever the other parent has died or is unknown or unavailable.

Following the thread of setting up preemptive immediate care for your children in the event of your death, you're going to want to set up some kind of **trust** to handle your property for your children in case you die. This can be done inside your will. An estate attorney can enclose a trust inside that will not be funded until after you die, or which could be funded with life insurance proceeds. You can direct future life insurance money into the trust.

You can also set up a living trust immediately, as I have discussed previously, putting your property into the trust while you are still alive. You would then name yourself as the beneficiary, until such time as you die, then everything passes through the trust to your beneficiaries and if your children are minors, to a trustee who will manage it for them until they come of age.

While you are making a Will and Powers of Attorney, you might consider making a written anatomical and organ donation, and you may want a **Self-Designation of Guardian** to specify who you would approve and who you would disqualify to be your guardian in case of future need.

There are many different documents to consider, depending on your situation and your assets as well as your desires for the end of your life and for your estate after your death. While most people tend to focus on specific items of property to go to specific beneficiaries, estate planning should encompass so much more.

If it all seems overwhelming, make an appointment and go talk to an attorney about it. Often, it is not as difficult as you may think. People often spend an hour talking with me, give me the names of people that they trust to manage their estate and care for the children, and are surprised that I don't need to see their whole financial portfolio if they know their estate is far less than any applicable estate tax. An attorney can guide you to the documents that you need so that you don't have to worry about which ones to choose.

As you create these documents, it is important to remember that as the years go by, you may need to update them from time-to-time as laws change or people die, and families grow. The more specific you are in giving specific items to specific people, the more often you will need to update your Will. Making a Will, or even a power of attorney is not a once-in-a-lifetime event. You cannot revise these documents by scratching out sentences or writing in revisions. You will need to make an entirely new document and sign before witnesses and a notary with the same formalities as the first one. Make sure your agents and executors know where to look for the most current documents.

Wills are written with many unique considerations that depend on your stage in life, which highlights why it is essential to keep updating your will as time passes. I remember one client who illustrated this point in a rather funny way. She told me that she needed to update her will. When I asked why, she said that her old will stated that in the event of her death, her son is supposed to go live with her sister. The problem was that when she wrote the Will, her son was a child but now her son was 42 years old and had his own house and kids. Besides that, her sister, with whom her son was supposed to live, had died and now lives in Heaven. I agreed that her son probably would not be happy with those terms in her Will requiring him to go to heaven immediately, and definitely, she needed to update her Will!

CHAPTER 7

DO PEOPLE NAME THEIR SPOUSE AS THE EXECUTOR OF THEIR ESTATE?

Most married people do name their spouse as the person to act on their behalf in the event of their incapacitation or death (aka, the "**executor**" of their estate). If you're leaving all your property to your spouse, it makes sense to make your spouse the executor, so that they're in charge of the estate. Notably, if you make them the executor of the estate, it is up to them to get everything transferred into their own name after you're gone, and they would be most qualified to draft an inventory of the estate and to identify estate creditors.

Unfortunately, sometimes the person who is left behind doesn't have financial sophistication, the ability to manage financial matters, or the ability to handle probating a will. It may be that when you made your first Will, your spouse was capable, but now that your spouse has become elderly, he or she no longer has the mental or physical stamina to manage the estate. In those cases, rather than naming your spouse as the executor of your estate, it may be better to name an adult child or a trusted third party as the executor. That third party can then take care of getting your property to your spouse. In any event, you should always name an alternate Executor in case the first person you name cannot serve for any reason.

These are things that you will want to discuss with your spouse ahead of time. There is always just an assumption that you're going to leave everything to your spouse and put your spouse in charge of your estate, but it doesn't have to be that way. There can be a lot of hurt feelings that come up if you decide not to put them in charge, for whatever reason, but sometimes it is nevertheless best to name someone else. If you don't want to discuss it with your spouse at this time, you may want to write a letter to explain why and keep it with your Will.

I've seen that happen in my office several times. A couple will be discussing their respective wills, and one of them will say, "I'm not going to put my spouse as the executor", and it's clear that this is the first time they've talked about it. The other spouse will sit there blindsided, obviously feeling very disrespected or hurt because they're not being named as the executor.

As the advising attorney in these situations, it is my job to address the issue sensitively, carefully, and helpfully. Usually, I will ask, "Why you would want somebody else to be in charge?"

The answers vary. It may just be because the spouse isn't particularly financially savvy, and somebody else would be a better person to handle investments or to manage a complicated business. Perhaps one party is in the early stages of Alzheimer's disease and while coherent now, may not be much longer. It could be a matter of both parties being in sub-optimal health, and neither really having the capacity to manage an estate on their own. Or it could be that the children from the first marriage don't get along with the second spouse. Often the reason is to protect the spouse from family squabbles. Occasionally, it becomes clear that one party is considering divorce or feels forced to make a Will, in which case there is a conflict of interest for me, and I must refer them to separate attorneys. I am careful to point out to everyone that your Will is your own private business, and you do not have to tell your spouse or children what you put in your Will before you die, if you don't want to. If you don't like the Will, you can walk out the door and revoke it immediately or make a new one to replace that one.

There are many reasons people give, and most are usually resolved between the parties, with an ultimate decision to appoint a third party as the executor of the person's estate. Usually, the third party chosen is somebody who is already familiar with the financial situation. It is important to note that this person does not have to be a relative or even a close friend.

In fact, I know one couple that named a bank to manage their estate because they just didn't feel like any of their adult children would be able to do it without getting all their siblings upset with them. Rather than having the family fighting and mad at each other, they just named an institution to be in charge. Other clients have named a bank as executor because they have outlived all their relatives and don't know anyone willing and able to do it. A bank trust department can probate the Will or manage a trust, but be aware that they do charge a fee and you should probably discuss it with the bank before you decide to use that bank as executor. Many banks will only handle large estates. Sometimes people are emotionally attached to a particular investment stock and they don't want it sold, but that is the first thing the Bank Trust Department will do in order to invest the money somewhere the bank thinks would be more profitable or with the companies that the Bank has pre-approved. I've had two different clients who chose not to use a Bank as Executor for that very reason. They did not want their stock sold after they died. Of course, unless the stock was going into a trust, once the stock was transferred to the beneficiaries, the beneficiaries could always sell it themselves.

In any case, these are definitely questions to think about before coming in for an estate planning session, rather than just assuming that you or your spouse is going to be the executor. In some cases, it may be that the spouses need to each consult with their own individual attorneys rather than having one attorney do both Wills.

If ever you feel that the person you are with is pressuring you to sign a Will that is not what you desire, let the attorney know in some way, whether by a note, email, telephone call, or ask to speak with the attorney alone, confidentially. Keep in mind also, that if the Will doesn't say what you really wanted it to say, you can always revoke it simply by making a new Will or tearing up the old one. You can hire another attorney the next day to write a completely different Will. Your Will can then be kept in safekeeping at the courthouse Probate Clerk's office or with someone else whom you trust, rather than at home.

Should Married Parents Set Up Plans for the Financial and Physical Care of Their Children, If One or Both Die or Become Incapacitated?

If you have a large estate, you should consider the possibility of setting up a living trust so that somebody automatically steps in as an agent to manage financial affairs for your minor children. If you have an estate that doesn't have any estate tax issues, it may be that you want a temporary trust set up in your Will until the children reach a certain age, or you may just need to have a guardian for them named in your Will.

There are two kinds of guardians in this context:

1. A guardian of the person.
2. A guardian of the child's estate.

Often, people name the same guardian to be responsible for the property for their children and also be in charge of helping to raise the children (i.e., making sure they have a roof over their head and that all of their needs are met physically). However, you can also name two different people to fill the two different guardianship roles: one person with whom the children live or who finds a place for the children to live, and one person who manages the children's finances. In either case, the person or people who you want to fulfill these guardianship duties in the event of your incapacitation or death should be named in your will.

Guardianships are also necessary sometimes for elderly or mentally incapacitated adults. I know a mother who has a severely autistic adult daughter. Her daughter lives in a facility with 24-hour care. The mother is Guardian of the Person only. That gives her legal rights to manage her daughter's care and the right to confer with doctors and staff which she would not otherwise have with HIPAA privacy laws because her daughter is legally an adult. However, the daughter is supported by government funds managed by the institution so that the mother is not the guardian of her daughter's estate. This relieves the mother of the duty and burden of accounting to the court financially, but allows her to maintain watch to be sure that her daughter is getting the care that she needs. Even as guardian of the person, though, she must still file an annual bond and report annually on the well-being of her daughter in a written report to the court.

Notably, guardianship designations in estate planning documents can be both positive designations and negative designations. That is, you can definitively say, "I want X person to be my guardian if I need one or the guardian of my children", but you can also say, "I do not want X person to be my guardian or the guardian for my children under any circumstances."

Also, you want to have a medical power of attorney for your children, so that someone immediately has the right to make health care decisions for your children if you and your spouse are incapacitated or dead.

In addition, you need to think about what age cut-off you want to set before the children are allowed to take over their own finances. There is a good deal of discretion that you can exercise here. You can make it so that they get their whole inheritance as soon as they turn 18, or you can spread it out a little, perhaps waiting until they have graduated college or turned a certain age (usually 24-25). You can also scatter the release of funds, such that they get a certain percentage of the money (say, for example, one-third of their inheritance) at a certain age, then you have to wait a few years before they get the next installment, then have to wait a few years before they get the last installment. This can help prevent a potentially immature young adult from spending all of their inheritance recklessly or frivolously at once. The hard part is finding a trustee who is willing to manage the trust after the child becomes an adult.

There are many different ways that you can plot out when the children would get their money to manage on their own. This depends largely on who your children are, specifically on their maturity level and their ability to handle their own affairs. If they are not yet old enough or mature enough to handle their own affairs, it involves a kind of estimate or projection of what age you believe they will be when they become capable of handling their own affairs by themselves. For some children, the trust needs to be managed for the rest of their lives, perhaps due to mental incapacity or drug or alcohol addiction.

If One Spouse Dies or Becomes Incapacitated, Are There Certain Documents to Address Who Will Handle Property and Assets?

Yes. Regarding medical documents, we have a federal law called **HIPAA** which protects the privacy of your healthcare information. There are some heavy penalties for violating HIPAA, and healthcare providers are extremely keen to avoid those penalties. As such, it is extremely important not to simply assume that a doctor is going to tell your spouse what they need to know regarding your health care.

In situations where you are unable to communicate—for example, if you are suffering from Alzheimer's or dementia, or are in a coma—HIPAA laws make it absolutely essential to have a medical power of attorney in place, specifically one that names your spouse as the person who has the ability to talk to your healthcare provider about what is going on with you. Whenever I draft a Medical Power of Attorney, I also prepare a HIPAA release as well, in case there are other close relatives whom you would want to be informed about your condition.

You also need financial powers of attorney in place, since financial institutions have similar privacy laws. If there are, for instance, retirement plans or other assets that are only in one spouse's name, financial institutions are not going to talk to the other spouse unless they have a power of attorney. This issue can also be handled with a living trust, depending on the situation.

Does A Person Need to Employ Financial or Legal Devices to Transfer Their Business to Their Children?

There are many small, family-owned businesses and many types of business entities. For example, a business may be a sole proprietorship, a partnership, a Limited Liability Company (LLC), or a corporation. An ongoing business may be publicly traded or closely held by family. The business may be passed to the next generation by trust, transfer of stock, family limited partnership, or membership in an LLC. With the transfer of ownership, there are tax considerations. Each situation is different, so it is very important to consult with an attorney and CPA to discuss all the aspects of your business in order to determine the best way to transfer ownership to the next generation. There are too many possibilities to list here and the tax laws change from time-to-time. One thing that is universal, however, is that a power of attorney is particularly useful and a fast way to make sure someone can keep the business running in the event of an unexpected incapacity of the owner.

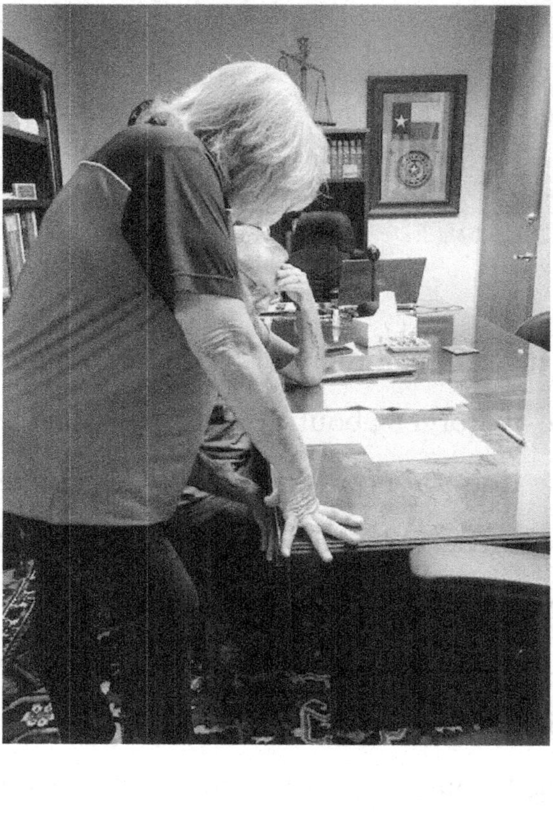

CHAPTER 8

DO DIVORCING COUPLES FORGET TO ADDRESS THEIR ESTATE PLANNING DOCUMENTS?

It's very common for a person in the midst of a divorce to forget about addressing estate planning, usually due to how emotionally overwhelming a divorce can be. Often, they feel uncertain whether they will own any property once the divorce is finished, and sometimes they are hoping for reconciliation or are just in denial that the divorce is happening. When a person is going through a divorce, they are concerned with many profoundly serious things at once. They are concerned with dividing their property and debts, as well as issues of child custody and how the divorce is affecting the kids. A lot of times, there is also a physical residential move involved, so they are concerned with the move itself. That means packing everything up, moving and dividing everything, and having to deal with everyone's emotions about it all.

In the midst of all of that, divorcing people are usually not thinking about updating their will. It takes some time and financial investment, it can be emotional, and it is just not fun. (Except to lawyers like me who enjoy writing wills). Even in the best of times, people tend to put off making a will and tell themselves that they'll get around to taking care of it later.

As someone who deals with these matters every day, I can tell you it is unwise to delay, even though it is understandable. Many people die in automobile accidents every day, even children, and almost none of those people planned on dying that day. You never know when you might get hit by a bus or you might have a heart attack out of the blue, even without any prior indication of health issues. We see more and more mass shootings and bombings where people of all ages are killed without warning.

This is even more noticeable today because of the pandemic. People are realizing that one day a person might seem perfectly fine, and then they might get COVID19 or have a heart attack, and then in just a few short days, they can be dead. It's very evident these days that life is short and unpredictable. This should highlight the fact that you simply can't put off your estate planning documents thinking that you're going to live forever. In the end, we can be sure that everyone is going to die one day. The only question is when, and no one knows exactly when.

So, yes, when you're in the middle of a divorce, it's important to have a new will made up as soon as possible. Who knows the nature of your property and the dynamics of your family more than your divorce attorney? Estate planning is something that people in the midst of a divorce often don't want to deal with, because they have too many other things taking up their time, money, energy, and emotional bandwidth. However, I have had several cases where a soon-to-be-ex-spouse died in the middle of a divorce, and without a will change, it was as if the divorce never happened. Unfortunately, in cases of domestic violence, the most dangerous time for the victim is when she takes a stand and files for divorce. Divorce is a time of great stress, but at the same time, it is imperative that she have a Will in place, for the sake of her children and parents, in case the worst happens.

It is a good idea to mention in a mediated settlement agreement that as of the day that the agreement is signed, all benefits conferred to the other spouse in a will or life insurance policy are revoked immediately, as a contract, rather than waiting until the divorce is actually granted.

It is understandable that most people are concerned about finances while in the midst of a divorce, particularly since the most common method of paying a divorce attorney is by the hour. This may be one reason a person is afraid of the expense of creating a Will, but a simple Will is usually done on a fixed fee basis, usually about the cost of one hour of the attorney's time, give or take a little. It is not nearly as expensive as a person in the midst of a divorce may fear, and it is money that can save their loved ones ten times as much time, expense and trouble later.

If A Divorce Is Imminent, How Should I Prepare My Estate Planning Documents?

I urge that you should make all necessary changes to your estate planning documents before your divorce is final. If you weren't able to make the changes or never got around to making the changes before the divorce was final, then certainly you should do it immediately after.

I should mention that there is a difference in the character of your property and how it is treated in Texas divorce and probate law based on when and how you acquired the property. In Texas, all property of a married couple is presumed to be "community" property, if it was acquired during the marriage, but there is such a thing as "separate" property. Separate property is something you owned before you married, or acquired by gift or inheritance at any time or something you receive as compensation for personal injury. In divorce, once a property is proved to be your separate property, the judge must award it to you, but you can give that same property to your spouse voluntarily in a settlement agreement or through a Will. In cases where someone dies without a Will, the law divides separate property differently from community property.

If you have a Will, you have total control over to whom you choose to leave your separate property and your half of the community, even though you are married. In Texas, you don't have to leave your spouse or children any property in your Will, not even one dollar. However, you can't give away your spouse's half of your shared community property. This becomes important if, say, you die in the middle of your divorce. In that case, even if you leave all your property to your children and you bypass your spouse, your children are only going to get half of the property, since half of it still belongs to your spouse. However, once your divorce is finalized, then a general statement such as "all of my property" in your will can give your children, or whomever you choose, whatever was awarded to you in the divorce.

Importantly, wills can be written in such a way that the divorce has little impact, so long as you know that the divorce is coming, and you plan for that when you write the will. An experienced divorce and estate planning attorney can help you with the details on that. But if you make no change to your old Will, then even though your ex-spouse may not receive the property, it is possible you may have chosen a different alternative Executor or Guardian for your children.

What If I Still Plan to Keep My Ex-Spouse as My Beneficiary and Designated Decision Maker, Including My Power of Attorney?

If you are one of those rare people who still trusts and cares for your ex-spouse and you want them to be your beneficiary even after divorce, you absolutely have to make a new will after your divorce, even if you want it to essentially say the same thing. The same is true for your power of attorney, your living trust, and your life insurance. This is because the law will presume automatically that you don't want your ex-spouse to be your beneficiary, or to be the person who makes financial decisions for you, or to be the person who manages your estate. If you keep the same will made during your marriage, both the life insurance laws, the Trust Code, and the Estates Code for wills will presume that you do not actually want your ex-spouse to be a beneficiary and/or executor. The Court and the life insurance company will skip over your appointment of your ex-spouse and go to the successor pretending as if your spouse had died before you.

Therefore, if you actually do want your ex-spouse to be the beneficiary and/or executor of your estate, you have to make a whole new will after the divorce is finalized. If you want them to be the beneficiary of your life insurance policy, you have to make a new designation of them as beneficiary on the policy, after the divorce is finalized. To do that, you must contact the life insurance company for a change of beneficiary form which is acceptable by that company. Life insurance is a contract between you and the company, so the Will does not control the life insurance policy.

As an aside, life insurance can be an exceptionally good tool for guaranteeing that child support will continue to get paid. If you have young children that you are helping to support and then you die, that could potentially devastate your children financially, since there is no more child support coming in. You can write in your divorce decree that if your ex-husband dies, his estate is still responsible for the child support, but whomever he has named as his new executor and beneficiaries are not likely to be very cooperative and collecting child support from the estate won't be easy. Even if your spouse promises to name the children as beneficiaries in his Will, there is no guarantee he won't change his Will and you won't know until he is deceased. Remember probate law is extremely strict and unforgiving, no one has to leave property to their children, and as you would be a creditor of the estate for child support, the Executor is likely to look for any legal means of avoiding your claim. However, if you plan ahead, your spouse can purchase a life insurance policy on his own life that provides money in the same way child support would, either to the ex-spouse outright or as a trustee for the benefit of the children. This is definitely something you should ask for in the mediation of your final divorce.

If you are planning to use life insurance to benefit minor children, you need to have a trust set up, because the life insurance money can't be paid out directly to the children until they are of age. Most commonly, you would set up the trust and name the parent who is collecting child support as trustee for the benefit of your minor children. You can create the trust in your Will or outside of your Will.

Otherwise, the life insurance company is going to require that legal guardianship be set up for the benefit of the minor child. Even though your ex-spouse is the other parent of the minor children, the life insurance company won't automatically payout to them on that basis. They'll require the parent to get a court order that says that they're the guardian of the children, which is expensive and a hassle, and may require your ex-spouse to put up a bond. In order to avoid all of that hassle, attorney's fees, and having to purchase a bond, you can set up a trust and name the parent, or another person, as trustee.

Things Divorced Parents Should Do When Changing Their Will to Prevent Ex-Spouse's Family from Becoming Their Children's Guardian

What if you don't trust your ex or his parents to do what is best for your children? After a divorce, it's always in the best interest of the children for the parents to get along well enough to communicate about things that affect the children. It would definitely be beneficial for the children for divorced parents to communicate and agree on who the guardian would be in both their respective wills, so as to avoid conflicting directions. It is a good idea to maintain a civil relationship with your ex-spouse's parents since they will always be your children's grandparents, but sometimes that just isn't possible.

Absent a court order, the law gives both parents total control as far as naming who they want to be a guardian or an agent on their behalf in the care of their minor children. So, the first thing you need to do is look at your divorce decree. There's a section in the divorce decree for the rights and duties of a parent. It will talk about which parent has the right to do certain things, like consenting to medical and dental, and psychological treatments, filing a lawsuit on behalf of their children, or consenting to one of their children getting married or joining the military while they are still minors. Depending on the divorce decree, these rights and duties and decision-making powers can be:

- Assigned exclusively to one parent or the other.
- Independently assigned, where each parent has the total right to do what they believe is best.
- Assigned primarily to one parent, with the provision that the parent must consult with the other parent first before they make any big decision.

Notably, most divorce decrees are silent on the issue of guardianship in the event of both parents' deaths. The District Court judge cannot appoint a guardian, since that is in the power of the probate court, so it is not going to be mentioned in your decree unless the spouses agree to put it in on a contractual basis. However, your divorce decree may say something specific about it or may hint toward one interpretation or another. An experienced attorney can take a look and help you figure it out.

Each parent can designate anyone they want to in their will though when it comes to the specific question of, "Who do I want to manage my children's estates and make sure that they have their physical needs met after my death."

I have seen many parents after divorce who say, "I do not want my ex-spouse to be in charge of my kids' well-being or their property." So in their will, they name a third-party guardian to take over in the event of their death. This is one of several areas where it is helpful to consult an attorney who practices both estate planning and family law. Many estate planning attorneys have little knowledge of the Family Code, and many Family Law attorneys choose not to get involved in cases governed by the Estates Code.

The surviving ex-spouse is still a parent. You can't terminate their parental rights in a Will, and they can still exercise those rights as a parent. However, if the deceased parent has appointed a guardian in their Will, that guardian would also have legal standing to challenge the actions and decisions of the parent in court. In a case like this, the guardian is the proxy for the deceased parent. If the deceased parent was the primary custodian of the children, the guardian they appointed in their will could therefore ask the court to make them the primary custodian of the children or at least to give them visitation rights so they can keep a close watch on the children.

If you have a situation where you really don't trust your ex-spouse to take care of your minor children, then naming a guardian would be a good idea. However, you want to make sure it's somebody who has the financial means and the emotional strength to challenge your ex-spouse in court. This would take a significant degree of strength and resources because it would be just like going through a divorce. It is an emotional and difficult thing to have a lawsuit over child custody. You may be setting up the person that you name as guardian to essentially have a child custody fight in court.

Most people do not realize how burdensome and expensive a guardianship is. You do not become a guardian simply because someone filled out a form or signed a Will or power of attorney. When you name a person to be a guardian in your Will, the court will honor your choice, but that person still has to qualify and prove that you need a guardian. It takes a court proceeding. An attorney must be appointed for the proposed Ward (the child), and if mental incapacity is an issue, a doctor must testify. There are multiple attorneys involved. The appointment of Guardian by a person is just the beginning. Once the court has signed an order appointing the Guardian, that Guardian must report annually to the Court and fulfill a host of other duties with Court oversight, including posting a bond annually.

For an adult child who may have limited abilities and special needs but some ability to communicate and make decisions, a guardianship might be avoided with a "Supported Decision-Maker" form which names a trusted adult who will assist the maker with important decisions. Sometimes, there is a designated payee of Social Security benefits who does not have to be a legal guardian, but they still have a duty to use that money solely for the beneficiary. In many cases, a power of attorney can help an adult avoid the need for guardianship. For a minor child, a **conservatorship** under the family code is often preferable to guardianship.

Grandparents' Rights in Texas

Increasingly these days it seems grandparents are raising their grandkids. Sometimes this is because one or both parents have died or are incarcerated. Other times, the parents might be struggling with addiction or mental illness. Sometimes it is a fluid situation where the parents of the grandchildren are unstable, and they float in and out of the children's and grandparents' lives. What rights do grandparents have to say, "enough is enough: for the safety of my grandkids, I'm taking control of them." The painful answer is that it is extremely difficult to do under the current state of our laws without the agreement of the living parents. The law presumes all parents are fit parents unless proven otherwise, and it isn't easy to prove otherwise.

A grandparent can step into the shoes of their own son or daughter who has died or had their parental rights legally terminated, but if the parents are still alive and have not had their rights legally terminated, the grandparents must prove that they even have a right to bring suit. The suit might get thrown out of court if they cannot meet the first hurdle of proving the right to bring suit based on their established relationship in the daily care of the child. Sometimes one of the parents has abandoned the child and the other is willing to agree, and sometimes child protective services may place a child with his or her grandparents.

It is not impossible, but it is very difficult to prove a parent is unfit. The law has a presumption that all parents are good parents until proven otherwise, and if at least one parent is fit, it seems the grandparents have no rights. Unless you can show significant harm to the children by a parent, often the grandparents are not allowed to bring suit unless they have already had exclusive control of the children for a certain period of time. Often the grandparent wants to have control of their grandchildren but doesn't want to have the parents publicly and legally declared unfit. Indeed, the lawsuit to that effect will severely damage the relationship between grandparent and parent.

On the other hand, the school may require more than a permission slip or power of attorney for the grandparent to enroll the child in school, and a health insurance company is going to require that the grandparent have legal status with a court order before they can insure the child on the grandparent's health insurance policy.

Grandparents often come to me seeking a guardianship of their grandchildren while the children's parents are still living. There are other legal means to accomplish the goal, and guardianship is almost never a good idea in Texas because it is the most restrictive and most expensive option. It is understandable that Grandparents think they need guardianship because the school and insurance companies often tell them that they must be the child's legal guardian when really what is needed is a legal duty to care for the child.

In order to get a guardianship in Texas, one must go through the probate court, pay for an ad litem attorney to be appointed for the children, prove why the guardianship is needed and what assets the children own, if any, and if appointed, post an annual bond and make annual reports to the Court for as long as the guardianship is in place. The same might not be true in other states, and I believe the term guardianship may have a different use or meaning in other states, but this is the rule in Texas. It is a burdensome and expensive process.

While the probate court has exclusive jurisdiction over guardianships, on the other hand, we can file a suit to establish a conservatorship, even for a non-parent, in District Court. A non-parent, whether or not a blood relative, can be appointed as managing conservator in certain situations, and have all the rights of a parent, including the right to collect child support from the parent(s) who might have only limited visitation rights.

This is a situation that often arises when grandparents take over the role of the parent. I have also used a conservatorship in a case where a mother died and the step-father had a close relationship with the child. The father of the child had not been close but did not want to have his rights terminated as would be required in order for step-dad to adopt the child. Still, the father recognized that the child needed to remain in the home where she had lived most of her life with the step-dad as primary caretaker for the child. The solution was to name the father and step-father as joint managing conservators, even though they lived many miles apart.

Likewise, it is not unusual for the court to order the grandparent and one or more of the parents appointed as ***joint managing conservators*** of the child, rather than making the grandparent a "guardian." That way the parent can still participate in the child's life, but the grandparent can act as parent legally, with all the rights and duties of a parent. That will also establish the grandparents' right to bring suit against the parents in the future, in some cases, for child support or for adoption. There is little to no court oversight of the grandparents after they are appointed as managing conservators, and they do not have to put up a bond. If a parent later turns their life around and is able to take more responsibility, a managing conservatorship can be modified, and custody can even be returned to the parent.

Alternatively, if the parent never visits nor pays any child support to the custodial grandparent, that may be used as evidence for termination of parental rights later. A managing conservatorship is a less expensive and less restrictive process than a guardianship all around and accomplishes the same goal of giving the grandparent the same rights as a parent.

JESUS CHRIST

CHAPTER 9

WHAT IS PROBATE UNDER TEXAS LAW?

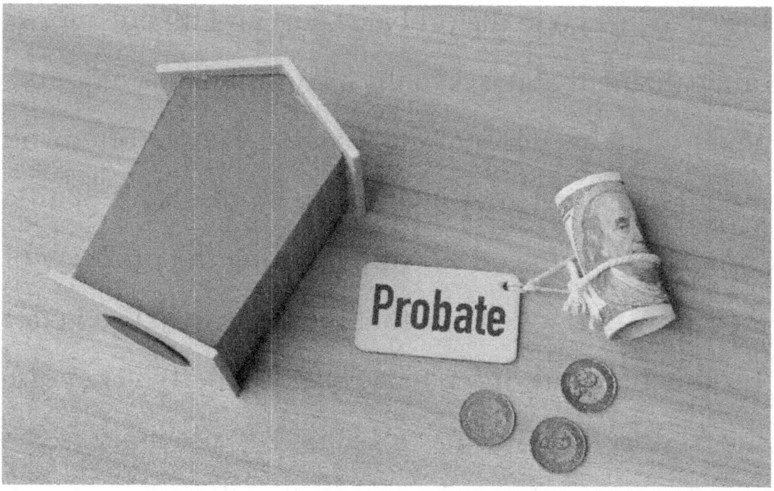

Probate has a broader meaning than most people realize. It actually refers to managing the estate of someone who is unable to manage their own estate or manage care for themselves, whether it is because of death, incapacity, or age.

Sometimes people ask if probate is somehow like "probation" which is a criminal connotation that has no relevance to this subject. Other times, people are told by a bank or title company that they need "Letters Testamentary" and they are confused thinking it is as simple as writing a letter, rather than what it actually entails which is filing a lawsuit. Many people assume they can just go to the probate court and fill out a form, not realizing that it is actually a lawsuit that is required, albeit often an uncontested lawsuit. People often call me and say that they were told by the bank or title company or some other entity holding the property of their deceased loved one that they "just need" a Letter Testamentary in order to get the property. They are shocked to find out that a Letter Testamentary is the certificate from the probate court that they can only get after they have probated a Will, paid a filing fee, posted notice, obtained a court order, and been appointed and qualified as the Executor of the estate. You cannot get a Letter Testamentary if you don't have a Will.

Sometimes people are needlessly afraid of probate when it may be a very quick and easy process in their situation with the help of an attorney. The probate process for the most part is not "user-friendly" but an attorney can often help make the process quick and painless. After filing various documents and obtaining a court order and being sworn in as Executor, then the probate clerk will issue "Letters Testamentary" which is an official certificate that certifies the Executor has been appointed by the Court and is authorized to manage the estate.

As we have discussed, in addition to the commonly understood probate to settle a dead person's estate, probate could also involve guardianship for a minor child who can't manage their estate under the law just because they're not yet 18 years old. It could also involve guardianship for an elderly person or young adult who can't manage their estate under the law because of mental incapacity.

"Estate" is another often misunderstood term. Your estate is your property of whatever kind. It is not just "real estate" or land. People often tell me that they have no estate, but when I start asking questions, they usually do have something. It may be a vehicle, a bank account, a retirement fund, jewelry, or just electronics and household goods, but if you own anything, you have an estate. In order to pass your property (in other words your estate), after you die to another person, you must have a Will, a Trust, or some other legal means which may involve a court proceeding.

When it comes to managing the estate of a deceased person, the first step is for someone to come forward and apply to be accepted by the court into an "executor" position (i.e., being in charge of the estate). There are two common misconceptions about the Executor. One is that people often think just because they are named as Executor in the Will that they are automatically in charge and all they have to do is show the Will to people as their authority to act. Another misconception is that as Executor, they can do whatever they think is best in deciding who gets what property from the estate. Neither is true.

If you have a will and you've chosen an executor, you need to make sure that the person you named knows that you have named them as the executor of your estate and knows where to physically find the ORIGINAL will in the event of your death.

They need to have a physical original will in order to execute the estate. Once the named executor finds an original will, (not a copy), the original Will gets filed with the Probate Court and a court hearing is scheduled. In this age of electronic filing, this is one area where the applicant or their lawyer still must take the original paper Will to the courthouse. Without an original, it is presumed that the Will was revoked, and the original is especially necessary if anyone suspects the Will might have been altered.

In some cases, I have been able to probate a photocopy as a lost Will, but it is more expensive, it requires witnesses, and it is not guaranteed to work, so the original is very important. Even if you have a very good photocopy, there must be a satisfactory explanation of what happened to the original.

If the deceased person did not leave a will, then the estate is called "intestate." Someone has to step forward and say, "I have an interest in this estate and I want to apply so that I can settle up the final affairs of this person." Then you have to determine who the deceased person's legal heirs are. Another attorney must be appointed by the court to represent unknown heirs. Thus, the person who wants to manage the estate is fronting the money to pay two attorneys, in hopes that after he or she is put in charge of the estate, they can get reimbursed from estate funds.

Several court proceedings are required just to get to the point of appointing that person to administer an intestate estate, and then they are required to pay for a bond, file an inventory and submit an accounting for the estate and be audited annually. That person, called an administrator rather than an executor, has to report back to the Probate Court on everything that they do for the estate. It is a big responsibility. Even when there is no contest and no debate on who should get the property, it is an expensive, lengthy, and stressful process without a Will.

For instance, when an *Independent Executor* named in a Will needs to sell the decedent's house, he just does it. He doesn't have to ask anyone's permission to list the house for sale and execute the documents to sell the house, deposit the money and distribute it according to the Will. But when there is no Will and an Estate Administrator is appointed, then the Administrator must have a court hearing to get a court order permitting him to list the house for sale, then get the court's permission to sell the house at a particular price once a buyer is located, then report back to the court once the sale is completed, and then pay an increased bond to cover the cash that just came into the estate. Then he needs still another court order on how to distribute or spend the cash proceeds from the sale. If the contents of the house are sold at an estate sale, or a vehicle is sold, there is a similar process and report of sale of personal property. Every trip to court requires a motion and order prepared by an attorney.

So, as a rule, it is a lot more complicated, it takes much longer, it is frustrating and it's a lot more expensive to put an estate through probate if you don't have a will. It is not the probate process itself that should be avoided, but instead what should be avoided is the situation called "intestacy" which is dying without a Will.

Either way, with or without a Will, the probate process isn't going to get triggered until somebody steps up and says, "I'm willing and qualified to manage this estate. I would like the Court to appoint me." If no one does anything, then eventually the State Comptroller will get the abandoned property, and the real estate may be foreclosed on to pay the property taxes.

What Complications Can Arise in Probate, If Someone Fails to Update Their Estate Planning Documents After a Divorce?

One major complication of not updating your estate planning documents after your divorce has to do with all the people that you have named throughout your will—whether it's the executor, a successor, an alternate executor, a trustee, a potential guardian for your minor children, or a beneficiary of your property. If any of those people are relatives of your ex-spouse, your relationship with them may have changed after the divorce, and you may not want them to occupy the same positions of responsibility when it comes to your estate.

When a person who's appointed in the will is related to the deceased person's ex-spouse, they may not be very cooperative and may not act in good faith. They may harbor hard feelings because of the divorce, as families tend to back the person that is related to them. Divorces tend to affect not just the divorcing couple, but also the entire familial community, including their extended family. Sometimes, even though a person doesn't trust their ex-in-laws, they want to keep a civil relationship because those same in-laws are their children's grandparents. It is difficult to do if one of the grandparents is also in charge of the estate and is slow to release needed funds. People tend to be less trusting when someone else is holding what they consider to be their money. You will often see a whole different side of someone you have known for decades. Emotions run high.

Estate planning documents and probate often indicate a change in title to a property. Whenever you get divorced, you need to have the title changed on those items (such as motorcycles, cars, houses, boats, etc.). If you don't change those titles of record, then there can be disputes over whether it belonged to the decedent or not, based on the divorce decree and the will.

Many times, people have left certain items to certain people in their will, and they don't even have that item anymore when they die. This can complicate things by causing accusations of someone stealing the item because it can't be found. The person who was supposed to get something, but gets nothing, feels cheated. After the decedent had an extended illness or after payment of all the debts, the estate may not be as large as the maker imagined it would be when they made the Will, so a gift of cash that was meant to be a small amount might be more than the estate has in total.

These are some reasons estate planning attorneys recommend using general terms like "I give all my property equally," or "I give 10% of my property…" so that a change in the specific property doesn't matter and the size of the gift can grow or shrink in proportion to the estate as a whole. Otherwise, every time you decide to sell or give away a piece of jewelry or something gets lost or stolen, you might have to make a whole new will to correct that specific gift in your Will. It takes skill to write a Will that plans for all the "what ifs." That is what an estate planning attorney is trained to do.

I'm Divorced. What Do I Need to do to Appropriately Update My Estate Planning Documents in Texas?

I highly recommend that anyone who is planning to make changes to their estate planning documents should first consult with an attorney. **Please don't try to "do it yourself!"**

There are many forms that you can find online, such as will forms and power of attorney forms. These days it seems you can find a do-it-yourself ("DIY")

YouTube or TikTok video for just about any project, Legal websites abound, and forms for Wills and for Divorces are plentiful online. However, you have no real way of knowing if these are even the right forms for Texas, if they are outdated, or if you are filling them out correctly. The laws are different in different states. Further, words may have a different legal meaning than the common everyday meaning that most people know. You may think you understand and not realize that you really don't understand. Remember that probate law is very strict, not just common sense. Probate law is the strictest area of the law, as far as judges having to do exactly what the law says, regardless of what you intended or what's fair. Therefore, you want to make extra sure that your will is valid under current Texas law.

You also have no real way of knowing if the form is actually up to date, which it needs to be in order to be fully valid and enforceable. Texas estate planning, will, and probate laws change from time to time, and forms you find online might have been perfectly valid 10 years ago, but are no longer valid today.

Again, you may think that I am discouraging DIY because I just want to make money, but truly I've seen many cases where it costs more money in attorney's fees to fix the mess that could have been avoided if the person had not tried to represent themselves. It is like trying to fix your own leaking pipes if you have no training in plumbing or fix the wiring if you know nothing about electricity. It will cost you much more in the end than if you had called the expert in the beginning. It isn't a matter of whether you are intelligent, but you have not spent years learning this skill. I've seen couples fighting in court who were divorced 20 years earlier and their property was never properly divided because they tried to write their own divorce decree, and many times I've seen DIY Wills rejected by the court. Expensive court battles can result over what the words mean because while it may make perfect sense to you, other people may find double meanings.

In the case of a Will, you won't know that the Will is no good during your lifetime. Your loved ones will pay the price after you die when it is too late to fix the Will. The only way to be absolutely sure is to hire an estate planning attorney to put your will together.

I recently saw a DIY will where the decedent had left all her property to her brother, named her brother as executor, but then ordered that the executor put up a bond to protect the beneficiary from any mishandling of the estate by the executor. In other words, the brother had to buy insurance to protect himself in case he embezzled from himself. I don't know whether the person who made the Will just accidentally left out the word "No" in front of the word bond, or if she didn't understand what a bond was for. That made no sense, and it was an unnecessary expense, but because the Will required a bond, then a bond was ordered. The judge had no choice.

It's not just a matter of which words are used. It's also a matter of how the document is executed. It must be signed in a certain order and by certain people. For instance, there are cases in the books where a Will was rejected because the witnesses did not watch the testator sign. Even though everyone signed in the right place on the Will, and the Will said all the right things, still the Will was thrown out.

In a case of emergency, where you are dying and have no opportunity to consult an attorney, a handwritten will might be better than nothing at all, but that is a rare exception. Even if all you do is name an independent executor, that would help your family, if it is a valid will. But your loved ones would be best protected if you hire an attorney to write your will. One of the most common mistakes I see with DIY wills is when a person types it, thinking that makes it more official, but without witnesses and a notary, the Will should have been handwritten entirely in the maker's own handwriting. I've also seen a father print a handwritten Will for his daughter to sign. That would not work because it was not entirely in HER handwriting. Even if you succeed in making a valid DIY Will, it is very likely that an attorney could have made your will in such a way as to avoid a pitfall you did not see.

I can't tell you how many times somebody has come into my office telling me their loved one has died and presented me with what they say is their loved one's will. Then I look at the document and it's not signed, or it's not signed by the right people in the right place, or it fails to name an executor. It's either totally invalid or very inadequate. What's worse, if that's your will, you won't know that it's invalid until it's too late to do anything about it, because you have already passed away. Other times, the Will can be probated, but it is much more difficult than it needed to be, and it is impossible to fix that once the person has died.

So, it's incredibly important to have an experienced attorney put together your will. Everybody needs a will. Even if you already have a living trust, you must also have a will—though make sure your attorney knows about your living trust, so they can write a will that can fit with the trust.

If you have a living trust and you're getting divorced, you definitely want to change that trust during the divorce process, or as soon as possible after the divorce is finalized. You want to get it changed so quickly because trusts don't go through probate. The judge won't be looking over the trust document to see if it makes sense after the divorce. If you have a living trust written during your marriage that presumes your spouse was going to get everything after you die, and you don't actually want them to get everything, you need to change that trust immediately. While the trust code says after divorce the law treats the divorced spouse as if they predeceased the decedent, banks don't usually ask if you have been divorced after the trust account was opened. They are not responsible to know that the written document is no longer valid. Not only do you need to put a revocation in writing, but you need to deliver a copy of that to every bank that was relying on the old document. There is most likely real estate and other property that is in the name of the trust that needs to be transferred out of the trust as well, so it requires more than just revoking the trust.

Likewise, if you previously named your ex-spouse as your agent on your Power of Attorney for financial matters, remember that the third parties which may be relying on that power of attorney have no way to know that the Power of Attorney has been revoked unless you tell them or your ex-spouse tells them. You need to be aware of the persons with whom your ex-spouse may have been doing business on your behalf, and notify them in writing that you no longer authorize your ex-spouse to be your agent.

And on the subject of an ex-spouse raiding a decedent's bank account or acting without your consent, all joint accounts should be closed as soon as possible after divorce, if not already done before, and you should change your PIN numbers and passwords on your debit and credit cards. Even if there isn't much money in the bank account, if your ex-spouse or soon-to-be-ex-spouse overdraws the account and it goes negative, you are liable for the deficit if you are a joint owner on the account.

CHAPTER 10

THE DILEMMA OF SECURING DIGITAL ASSETS

The dilemma of Securing Digital Assets. Let's unpack that title a little. What are your digital assets? Online bank accounts, apps, cryptocurrency, and anything of value that you may own online. It could include a site that you have created or a blog that has advertising income and could be sold. The dilemma of digital security is that while you're alive you want to protect your digital assets and keep them secure from hackers, but once you die those same protections may make it difficult to find crucial information needed to execute your estate. The more secure something is, the less user-friendly it is.

If you are in the process of getting divorced, there are also certain protections you will probably put in place to protect your digital assets from your soon-to-be-ex-spouse. There's a lot of identity theft that goes on during divorce, unfortunately. Therefore, digital security measures may be necessary to prevent your ex-spouse from, say, reading your emails, or intercepting emails between you and your attorney, or even sabotaging your finances by getting into your bank account and changing things online. All those things that could happen to you are illegal, of course, but they still may leave you broke.

At the same time, once you pass away, all those things that you put in place to guard your privacy and digital security may become severe hindrances. Your executor will need to get past your digital security measures to access things like your bank information or even the balance owed on your mortgage. These days, your bank account notices and brokerage account information are generally all online and sent via email or text message, so since no statements come in the mail, the executor may not even know you have that account. Your bills get paid automatically out of your bank account online, or at least you get your bills sent to you through your emails. If you wanted someone to take down your Facebook page or your other social media accounts, all those things have passwords too. Therefore, your online financial account passwords and social media accounts, your blogs, your YouTube accounts, would all need to be accessible by your executor, but secure from everyone else.

A lot of things now have 2-Step verification, where not only you do have to have the password, but they send a code to your phone. This brings up the issue of the phone itself. In the 2-step verification, your executor may need to access your phone so they can get the verification code and then use that password to get into the accounts that they need to get into. If your phone has a lock password on it, and you were the only one who knew the password, how will your executor get past the lock code to open your phone? There might also be other essential information stored on your phone, past that initial password and sometimes even past additional password protections.

In order to do your banking and to take care of your finances and your emails, the executor of your estate will need to know all your passwords. They need to have access to your phone, your email, your bank account, your social media accounts, and all your most sensitive information, which are the very things that you generally have tried to prevent hackers (or your ex-spouse) from getting into.

So, there's the dilemma of making this information accessible to the right people once you die, but not while you're still alive.

As a potential solution, you may put some of those codes and passwords in writing and put that document with your will. However, if you get divorced, you will want to make sure that your ex-spouse doesn't get ahold of those passwords and access codes once they've been written down. If you have written down a sort of "cheat sheet" for your passwords and your ex-spouse has had access to the will (and the accompanying cheat sheet), you should change all those passwords, because your spouse may have already had access to them or at least may be able to guess them. If you hide the password cheat sheet too well, your Executor may not be able to find it, but if you have the cheat sheet in an obvious place, someone else that you do not trust might see it. Also, if you have a paper list of passwords, you will need to update it every time you change a password.

I recommend that you have one of those master password apps, where all your passwords are stored electronically on a secure site. That way, your future executor will only need one password to get into the app, and therefore to access the rest of the passwords. The app will also make it easier for you to update passwords whenever you change them, and you will always have the passwords on your phone so you are less likely to forget the passwords yourself.

Beyond the issue of passwords, digital or virtual assets are also a factor to consider. Cryptocurrency and intellectual property are other aspects of estate planning that you want to be sure your attorney and your Executor know about. If your Will simply says "I leave all my property to x," how will the executor know that your property includes Bitcoin or other cryptocurrencies? What if you have an unfinished book, movie script, invention, or scientific formula that might be marketed? What if you have a website, blog, Pinterest, Air B&B, an app you created, or other accounts that could be sold? These assets may be hard to find, especially if no one close to you knows that they exist or where to look for them. You must communicate those things to your Executor before you die. It is a good idea to leave some written instructions along with your Will to let the Executor know that these things exist and have value. Perhaps put the instructions in a safe deposit box.

CHAPTER 11

ESTATE PLANNING IN SECOND MARRIAGE AND BLENDED FAMILY

Blended families refer to situations where people with children from previous marriages remarry, and they have his kids, her kids, and our kids. If you have a blended family, it's especially important to have a will. In a blended family situation, if you pass away without a will, everything's going to be tied up while those kids are minors. And if you consider all your kids to be equally "our kids" and you want them all treated the same, they are not going to be treated the same for inheritance purposes unless you have a Will. Sometimes, sadly, people become estranged from the kids from prior marriages, and sometimes, even though you have a good relationship with your kids, you don't want them to inherit anything from you while your second spouse is still alive.

The Will is even more important in blended families to ensure that the second spouse will be able to sell the house if needed. For example, let's say there's a blended family, and one of the spouses dies. It may be that the surviving spouse really can't afford to make the house payments without the deceased spouse's income. If the house was bought during the second marriage, it is community property, half-owned by the surviving spouse. However, the surviving spouse might not be able to sell the house, because the deceased spouse's minor children from a prior marriage automatically own part of the house since their father did not leave a will. Some of those minor children may have a different mother, who may not cooperate with a second wife (i.e., the surviving spouse). In other cases, a guardian may have to be appointed to represent the minor children and do what's best for them, so there may be a guardianship court proceeding in addition to having an intestate estate in probate court. Even if the kids are adults, they want to be compensated when the house sells. Often, these situations end with the house being foreclosed on by the mortgage company or sold for property taxes because of the complication of having multiple owners who may not get along or agree on what to do.

All this turmoil can be avoided by simply having a will that says, "I leave my house to my spouse (name)," rather than doing nothing. Without a Will, the law will default to a part of the house belonging to your children from your first marriage.

It's important not only to have a will, but to have a will put together thoughtfully by someone who can spot blind spots. For instance, let's say a person has a will that was written after their first divorce that says, "I leave everything to my three kids." If they remarried but never changed their will, it means that they have left out that second spouse entirely. The second spouse isn't going to get anything from the deceased spouse's estate because we don't presume that you would have updated your will after you got married. The law presumes that you don't want your ex-spouse to inherit, but it doesn't presume that you do want your second spouse to inherit. All that the second spouse is entitled to, is half the property that was earned during the marriage, which is community property.

Therefore, you definitely want to update your will if you remarry. Also, if you have children who were born after your standing will was made, and you die before changing it, that can really mess up your whole estate plan. For instance, if you left everything to your current spouse, but then you have another child, then that child may get half of your estate. Meanwhile, the children you had before that child don't get anything, because you left everything to your current spouse. This can obviously cause an enormous amount of pain, complication, and turmoil, all of which you can avoid by simply making a new Will promptly after you remarry and/or after you have more children, even if you don't change a word.

Speaking of children born after a Will is made, it is important to acknowledge in a Will any child born out-of-wedlock or due to an affair. It may be that is an uncomfortable topic, but there are many cases where after a person dies, someone appears who claims to be the biological child, born outside of the decedent's marriage, and they may be entitled to a portion of the estate. It is not uncommon for a person to die without a Will, have a child who is not the child of the widowed spouse, and much money is spent in litigation over the rights of that child to inherit. There is a presumption in family law that a child born during a marriage is the child of the husband, but the presumption can be rebutted with genetic testing. If the decedent doesn't want the child to inherit, he or she needs to acknowledge in the Will that the child exists and affirmatively state that the child is not to receive any portion of the estate. You can disinherit any relative, but make it clearly intentional.

Do Assets Need to be Re-titled in Both Names in A Second Marriage or Should an Individual Leave Some Assets in Their Name Only?

I recommend that people leave some assets in their name only, if they have a valid up-to-date Will. Our community property laws say that anything you get by gift or by inheritance is your separate property, and anything you owned before the marriage is your separate property. However, you must prove it's your separate property, as the law presumes that everything is community unless you can prove with documentation that it's actually separate property.

So, if you get divorced, the judge awards you a certain amount of property that is your separate property. If you get remarried, even to the same person, the property that you owned before the marriage, which was assigned to you by a judge in your first divorce, is your separate property. If you owned property before you married or inherited property, that is also your separate property, as are your personal injury damages.

If you re-title your separate property, sign a new deed, and put your second spouse's name on the deed, then you're not actually creating community property. What you're actually doing is giving your new spouse half of your house as their own separate property, because you're making a gift to them. It is possible to convert your separate property to community, or vice versa, in a written document, but you should check with a lawyer to make sure it is done properly because simply putting the other person's name on the title or making a gift is not enough to convert it.

The judge must award separate property to the person whose name is on that property. So, if you get divorced from your second spouse, the judge must award you your half of the house and has to award them their half of the house. This will probably mean that you're going to have to sell the house. Generally, going that route takes away a good deal of flexibility in the division of all the property and debts, and if you were the one who came into the marriage with the house, you might not be happy if you are forced to sell.

A better solution would be to put a stipulation in your will that your surviving second spouse will get the house when you die. That way, if you're married, you're going to make decisions together about the house. If you decide to sell the house, you both must sign at the closing of the sale anyway because of our Texas Homestead Laws. If you don't decide to sell the house and you die before your spouse, then your spouse gets the house through your Will. Even if you give ownership of the house in your Will to someone else, such as your adult children, your surviving spouse still has the right to continue living in the homestead after you die if that was the spouse's homestead at the time of your death. If you get divorced from the second spouse, everything is a lot less complicated if you have not put their name on the title to your separate property (in this case, the house). Then the judge must award you the house that you brought into the marriage. You can always change your Will if your relationship changes, but it is not so easy to take back a gift deed while you are alive. So the Will protects your surviving spouse if you die, but doesn't hurt you if you get divorced from that second spouse. A valid, well-written Will is the key.

Besides a Will and Other Documents, What Other Estate Planning Tools are Necessary in a Second Marriage to Avoid Probate Issues?

You should review your powers of attorney after you re-marry. For instance, if you were hospitalized and incapacitated, you would want your doctors to be released from HIPAA privacy laws to talk with your second spouse about your medical condition. You will probably want to have that second spouse listed in your medical power of attorney, or at least on a HIPAA release, for that to happen. Imagine if the medical power of attorney on file still listed your former spouse as the person with the right to discontinue your life support. If you don't want your current spouse to have that power, you certainly don't want your former spouse to have that power.

You will also want to add your current spouse to your statutory power of attorney for financial decisions. For instance, you will want to make sure your new spouse is able to access accounts that might be in your name only so that they can pay the bills if you're not able to pay the bills because you're incapacitated. If you're a small business owner and you are the only person able to sign company checks, you will need to give someone a power of attorney to make sure your employees and the IRS get paid if you are unable to function. So, you definitely want to update both your medical power of attorney and your financial power of attorney, as well as update your will.

Next, check your life insurance policies to make sure you have the person you want to have listed as a beneficiary. If not, you must get a form from the insurance company to change beneficiaries.

After that, just look at everything else that you have in the way of estate planning documents, such as your designation of an agent to control your remains for cremation, your self-designation of guardian, and who you've named in your medical power of attorney to make decisions for your minor children. You want to make sure that the people that you named are still the people that you want now that you have remarried.

SECTION III

What If We Don't Plan Ahead?

CHAPTER 12

What Happens If You Fail To Plan?

Life will go on if you don't plan, but planning definitely makes things better for your future and the future of your family. A Will and life insurance can make a dramatic difference in the outcome of your family's finances. The younger you are, the less expensive the life insurance.

If you sign off on a divorce decree without understanding it, or worse, if you are served with a divorce petition and ignore it, you will probably get divorced even without your participation. You can't stop a divorce by ignoring it. However, in the case of a default divorce, you could lose all your property and more. I've literally seen default divorce decrees that award the house to the Petitioner and all the debt to the Respondent, including the mortgage. Even though the house is your homestead, your ex-spouse may evict you if the court awards the house to your ex. You may be ordered to pay spousal maintenance or child support that is more than would have been ordered if the judge knew all the facts.

For example, I know a man whose wife lied about physical disabilities for herself and his daughter at a default divorce. By the time he came to see me, he had been paying spousal maintenance for 23 years to his ex-spouse who had no right to statutory post-divorce maintenance because she had every ability to work, and she even ran marathons. Even more outrageous, money was still being withheld from his pay for child support and being sent to his ex-wife for his 40-year-old (supposedly disabled) daughter who was married and working as a nurse. His daughter wasn't getting the money; his ex-wife was getting it. She was building herself a brand-new mansion with his maintenance money and child support while he struggled to pay his own rent and worked two jobs.

In another case, a woman I represented had signed a decree that her ex-husband had drafted, and she had been missing out on half her ex-husband's retirement pay for 20 years because retirement was never mentioned in their divorce decree. No one does any fact-checking on a default order.

On the probate side, in the case of a person who dies without a Will, the family may simply lose whatever money the deceased had in his bank account, or the surviving family may spend thousands on attorney's fees that would have not been necessary if the deceased had ever bothered to do a simple Will. It is common to hear of families who have lost the family farm to pay estate taxes which could have been completely avoided with a living trust or LLC. Even modest homes have been lost because too much time has passed without probating a Will and too many children, grand-children, and great-grandchildren who all had a claim to the house could not agree on selling the property. Houses may be sold just to pay ad valorem taxes and bank accounts sent to the State Comptroller as abandoned property because it is too expensive to probate the intestate estate, and then the heirs get nothing.

In cases where a person becomes incapable of managing their own physical well-being and/or financial affairs, such as in cases of Alzheimer's, dementia, or coma, if there are no medical and statutory powers of attorney in place, then a guardianship may be the only possibility. This means that the estate will pay for a doctor to certify that the person is incapacitated, pay for an ad litem attorney to represent that person, and there must be service by a process server on the person and an evidentiary court hearing. Once the court determines the extent of the incapacity and need for assistance, if the only property owned by the person is community property, then the spouse can be appointed community administrator, but if there is separate property, a guardianship is necessary and that means an annual bond premium.

Unless there is an advance directive in place to give direction on life support, doctors will do everything possible to keep a person alive, while leaving the family with a mountain of medical bills even when there is no hope of recovery. I've seen surviving children in agony because they couldn't financially afford to hire an attorney to get a court order so that they could cremate a body or transport a body to a burial site when a simple document from the decedent would have made a court order unnecessary. Also, organ donations are wasted if no one knew that the deceased wanted to donate his or her organs.

In the case of a medical condition for which there is no hope of recovery, doctors are trained to never give up, but eventually, someone from the hospital or hospice may ask your family if they are ready to consent to removing your life support. This is a difficult and guilt-causing decision for a loved one to make at a very emotionally-vulnerable time. It also leads to terrible arguments among family members. I have often heard people accuse other members of their family of murdering their loved one, when in fact they did what they thought was best under the circumstances and it was legal. When the family can't agree and there is no written directive from the patient, the hospital will submit the decision to the court and the estate will pay the legal fees. Many a court battle has resulted between those who claim that mom or dad "would not have wanted to live that way," while others claim it is best to keep them alive at all costs because "where there is life, there is hope." A directive to physicians or even a medical power of attorney could have spared the family the financial expense and years of bitterness.

The same is true for cremation. I've seen court battles where half the family says that mom or dad's religious beliefs would have never allowed them to be cremated, while the other half of the family claims that is what mom or dad told them they wanted. Half of the family accuses the other half of only caring about spending the estate money for a burial. It can get very ugly, and criminal charges may result. Then there is the question of what to do with the ashes or cremains. In cases of divorce, as well as will contests, there have been court battles over who gets the urn with a loved one's ashes.

If you have a blended family with minor children, the unexpected death of a biological parent could lead to the breakup of the family if the ex-spouse steps in. I've represented surviving stepparents where the ex-spouse of the deceased is totally out-of-the-picture and the child thinks of that stepparent as their parent, but a relative of the ex-spouse files for custody because they are a blood relative of the child. Again, some planning could save the surviving spouse, child, and other siblings and step-siblings much grief.

One woman I represented wanted to adopt her half-sister when their mutual father passed away. The mother's rights had been terminated for child abuse years before, so the young child did not remember any of her maternal relatives, but the maternal grandmother fought for custody. The father had written a note stating that he wanted the half-sister to take care of her younger sibling, but that note was not a legal document as would have been a designation of a guardian or a Will or a conservatorship, and it was not allowed into evidence.

The bottom line is failure to plan could result in a terrible emotional legacy for your family and could financially harm the next generation.

CHAPTER 13

THINGS YOU SHOULD DO THAT DON'T INVOLVE A LAWYER

First, set aside a time on your calendar when you will take the first steps. Make a plan. Get some phone numbers, make some calls, and set some appointments to see an attorney, financial planner, counselor, realtor, etc. You can ask for recommendations from NextDoor app or Facebook, check reviews online, ask a friend, or ask your attorney to recommend other professionals. Make a list of what you plan to do, write it down, and set yourself some deadlines. Make an appointment with yourself to spend an hour on it each day. If you are planning a divorce, make yourself a budget for life after marriage. In order to reach a big goal, it helps to have some smaller, incremental goals. If you are planning a Will, think about who you would want to be your executor, child's guardian, an agent on a power of attorney, and an alternate person for each role. Outside of the Will, who do you trust to be your privacy guard? (I'll tell you more about the privacy guard a little later on).

If you have a Will, make sure the person you named as Executor, as well as the alternate executor, know that they are appointed in your Will and where to find the original Will. Many times, the family believes that a Will was created, but they cannot find it. The grieving family has many tough decisions to make and life for them is forever changed, so the process of searching for a Will that they cannot find is extremely stressful.

Make sure that your Executor knows that the Will must be probated before it becomes valid. Many a person has assumed that all they needed was the Will to put them in charge of the estate, not realizing that the Will has no effect until it is approved by the Court. And many a person has assumed that they own a house because the Will left it to them, but they never bothered to probate the Will, or worse, they assumed it just automatically became theirs by marriage. When it comes time to get a home equity loan, refinance, or sell, they can't do it because title hasn't been cleared.

The best time to come see me is within a few days after the funeral. The Will need not be probated before the funeral, and you will have plenty to do and extended family to visit with until then, but you can call to make an appointment for a date soon after the funeral. It is helpful if you can bring a death certificate with you, but sometimes it takes a few weeks to get those, and you can bring it later. As soon as possible after the funeral, you should get started on the probate because you will need to be appointed as Executor in a court hearing before you can manage the estate, and soon after you will need to complete an inventory of what the decedent owned on the date of his or her death. That inventory becomes more difficult to do as time goes by.

Carefully consider how the family will pay for the probate of the Will and how they will manage living expenses until the Will is probated. Any bank account that is not expressly a joint account will be frozen by the bank until the Will is probated. All powers of attorney are immediately void when the maker dies. However, a surviving co-owner of a joint account with the right of survivorship immediately owns the account and can continue to use it. Not all joint accounts have a right of survivorship, although most do. A joint account with the right of survivorship will override a Will, so you may not want to make all your accounts joint with an adult child or other non-spouse executor, because that could lead to a vastly different distribution of property than you had intended with your Will. On the other hand, at least one account with enough money for the funeral and probate expenses would make the financial burden easier to bear for the person making those arrangements. You can make your account joint by signing a form at the bank. If you aren't sure what the status of your accounts are, this is a good time to contact the bank and find out whether the co-owner has a right to survivorship.

Stored with your Will, keep an inventory list of your bank accounts, life insurance policies, safe deposit boxes, and credit accounts, with account numbers. Other legal documents that should be either copied and kept with the Will or a list detailing where the document can be found include Divorce Decrees, Rent Receipt books for any rental homes that the decedent may own, receipt books showing any direct payments of child support or alimony, Deeds, social security card, government benefits, reverse mortgage documents, personal injury annuities, payout information of lottery winnings that are paid out over time, and pension and retirement fund paperwork. If you have a large amount of these papers, you may want to put them on a flash drive or make copies and put in a notebook.

As previously discussed, along with your Will, keep an updated list of your passwords, access codes, and the answers to your security questions, and some instructions about what you own and where to find it. Or better yet, keep a sealed envelope with the Will that tells the executor the password to your cell phone and the app that stores all your passwords.

Your cell phone can be a great tool for your Executor to find contact names, phone numbers, and sometimes even addresses for people who should be notified. However, it is no help at all if it is locked and no one knows how to unlock it. Also, Wills usually don't have contact information for the beneficiaries, and if you have left specific items to multiple people, a list with the contact information of your beneficiaries might be very helpful to your executor when it comes time to make the final distributions. I once represented an executor for a woman that left a generous sum of money to an estranged daughter who was last known to live in Hawaii. We searched and searched for the daughter, but in the end, had to give the daughter's property to the State as abandoned property because we could not locate her. An address book would have been helpful. If you can't find your own beneficiary, then how do you expect your executor to find them?

Besides the papers that you should keep handy, there are some things you may want to dispose of. Appoint someone as your PR person, secret-keeper, digital executor, or "Privacy Guard," to make sure that embarrassing things are cleaned up or deleted when you die. This needs to be someone you trust with all your secrets, not necessarily your Executor although it can be the same person, and you should put something in writing informally in case other family members question the authority of the Privacy Guard's actions. Privacy Guard is not a legal status, it is just a term that I coined to describe someone you trust with your secrets. That person needs to realize that they cannot destroy any important legal documents, only embarrassing ones that have no legal effect after the owner's death. Hopefully, it is someone who is experienced in using the internet, but there are paper documents to be considered as well.

I'm talking about old love letters which might be explicit or evidence of an affair, embarrassing photos, and such.

Think about items that might be found on your laptop or phone after you die that could be hurtful or embarrassing. Either have your Privacy Guard find and erase those things, or have that person destroy the hard drive. The Privacy Guard may have to smash the hard drive with a hammer to make sure it is truly erased, and they need some proof that they had permission to do that. He or she may need to do even more if it is on the internet. But make sure that there is no information on the laptop that the executor needs, such as passwords, contact information, or bank account information before you go to extremes. Photos and text messages on a cell phone might need to be erased, but the phone itself is not destroyed because of the access it provides to financial accounts.

Think about your social media. Do you want all those family photos and your opinions and posts to be left as they are? Do you want people who may not know you have died to continue to try to contact you through social media? Some people choose to keep their social media accounts open as a "memorial." Others want the accounts erased completely when they are gone. Google "digital legacy" for more ideas. Apple and Facebook have explicit instructions. It would be helpful to look at the bookmarks on your computer and the apps on your phone and make a list of all your online accounts, and especially leave instructions to close any shopping accounts such as Amazon.

Your Privacy Guard may need to get rid of some documents as well. Perhaps you have kept evidence that you were arrested once long ago, or that you were treated for a sexually transmitted disease long ago. Medical records, court documents, letters, evidence of an affair, pornography, and such may not be something you want your kids to see. Perhaps you have a diary or journal that would only cause hurt if anyone read it. You may want your Privacy Guard to find and destroy those documents, whether on paper or online.

If you really want to help your family, you could write your own obituary and choose photos for your funeral or memorial service. As I stated before, there is much to be done in a brief time with little prior notice for most funerals. It is difficult to summarize someone's life in a few paragraphs and no one knows better than you what you want to be remembered about your life. Rather than leaving your family to sort through photographs and try to remember dates, names, and accomplishments, help them out with this part of the process.

Planning ahead requires some thought, time, and work on your part, and communication that is sometimes difficult is essential, but your loved ones will be most appreciative that you did it. It is one of the best gifts you can leave to your family.

CHAPTER 14

WHEN SHOULD DIVORCING OR DIVORCED COUPLES CONTACT A LAWYER?

Anytime you're considering divorce, you should come in for a consultation. Even if you don't hire me, everything you tell me is confidential by the rules of professional responsibility. All attorneys are required to keep the things that you tell them confidential in a consultation, even if you don't hire them to be your attorney. So, if you are considering a divorce and you have pressing questions, I can do my best to help you in a way that is guaranteed to be confidential and safe.

Keep in mind that a lawyer can only represent one side in a divorce, not both husband and wife. Couples sometimes come together and say they want to hire the same lawyer to handle their divorce. That would be unethical for any lawyer to attempt because, by its very nature, divorce is adversarial, even if the parties are in complete agreement. If both husband and wife have already agreed on every issue, I must tell them that they have to decide which one is going to be my client and the other one must realize that they are representing themselves as if they were a lawyer. It must be clear from the start which one I owe a duty of loyalty to, and which one is a self-represented litigant.

I often have people come to these consultations asking me what will happen to their house, and specifically what will happen if they decide to leave their house. I hear that a lot of people are afraid that if they move out of their house, it will count as an abandonment of the property, and they will cede their rights to the house. This is simply not true in Texas.

You still have an ownership interest in your house, even if you are not physically living there.

Many people come to me with questions about how they go about separating their bank accounts, or how they can best protect their children, or how they can make sure they don't lose their ownership interest in their house, vehicle, or other property. If you are curious about these things, and about anything you might want to know about divorce, just come and talk to an attorney. Find out how expensive it's going to be and think about your budget, how much child support you are likely to receive, and how you're going to manage on your own before you file for divorce.

You don't have to be totally ready to pull the trigger on divorce to come and see me for a consultation. I am not going to pressure you into filing for divorce if you are not ready, although if you are in a domestic violence situation, I will urge you to get help. If the marriage can be saved, I encourage you to get counseling and be certain that you did everything possible to save it before you file for divorce. It is better than wondering later if you did the right thing. Often people come in to talk to me and get the information they need, then I don't hear from them for a while. Then, maybe 5 or 6 years later, they come back and say, "Now I'm ready to get divorced." It's not unusual at all for people to reconcile or try to work it out one last time. These things take time.

Also, just because you talked to an attorney doesn't mean you have to file a divorce right away. There is no obligation or pressure to move forward if you are not ready to do so. However, it is always good to be as informed as possible about your options and how to best protect yourself and your interests.

So, I would say as soon as you are considering divorce, just go get information to get the lay of the land and to help fill in the dots on your questions.

John Heard, Laura Heard, Marta Torres, Tonya Barton

What Sets the Laura D. Heard Law Firm Apart in Guiding Clients Through Divorce, Estate Planning, or Other Family Law Matters?

One thing that my firm is really good at is being compassionate and helping people through a really difficult time in life. Another thing to keep in mind is the experience level of your attorney. I have had the experience of representing a lot of different people in a lot of different walks of life and through a lot of different court experiences.

For instance, I represented "The Quad Mom" in San Antonio. She had given birth to quadruplets and was in the news for that reason a few times, then later she was in the news because she was murdered by her ex-husband, Allen Blackthorn. I had set up a trust for her children's child support and helped her in custody fights against Allen Blackthorn. Later, there was a True Crime book written about her after Allen Blackthorn was convicted of murder in federal court.

On another occasion, I represented the grandparents of the McFarland's children. There was quite a bit of TV coverage and another True Crime book written about them. Mr. McFarland murdered his wife during the holidays, and it took quite a while before her body was found. There was a big custody battle in the extended family over what would happen to his children when he went to prison. I represented the paternal grandparents in that case in children's court as they fought for access to their grandchildren.

I've represented a movie star in a contested probate matter, and I've represented hundreds of children who were living in foster care.

I've dealt with Child Protective Services and the Children's Court, the Probate Courts, the Criminal Courts as well as the Divorce Courts. All of that experience gives me a different perspective. I know how these things interact and intersect with one another. Compare this to an attorney who does only divorces, who may not really know how that's going to affect a probate situation or an attorney who does only probate, who is not really qualified to advise you on how to deal with a divorce situation. The experiences that I've had over the years help bring that all into play.

I also have the privilege of working alongside the outstanding staff that I've accumulated to work with me, who also brings a wide range of experience—as well as a deep understanding of empathy and compassion—to the table. We want to always be good listeners and be willing to help people who are going through something that is very difficult and emotional for them. I make sure that everyone that works here understands that we're dealing with people who are going through some of the hardest times of their life. Other firms may be just looking at the business aspect of how to divide things up, and what the law says. They try to move as many cases as possible, as fast as possible, and may even have non-attorneys handling the initial consultations. To many attorneys, they want clients to only think about the most financially favorable outcome, while I realize that sometimes relationships are more important, not just between soon-to-be ex-husband and wife, but also with the children, step-children, in-laws and grandparents.

At my firm, we're more willing to listen to what you're going through, realizing that everybody's situation is unique. Everybody has something in their lives that makes them a little bit different from everybody else, and the same is true for legal cases. In my firm, we are willing to take the time and really get to know the unique details of your case, so that we can try to do what is best in your particular situation. In some cases, we have been able to finish the divorce in 61 days, start-to-finish. In others, we have contested temporary orders hearings and multiple mediations if that is what is needed. We offer several options, not a cookie-cutter approach.

Well, did you learn something new in this book? I hope that this book has been helpful in educating you about some of the issues to consider and documents you should discuss with an attorney, and the terminology you need so you can ask the right questions. I hope you are inspired to make some plans, make sure your Will is up-to-date or that you will make it a priority to create a Will soon. Thank you for reading this book all the way to the end. For more information, check out my YouTube channel. I leave you with some photos of my firm. We hope to see you soon.

LDH™ LAURA D. HEARD LAW FIRM INC LDHEARD.COM

- *Check out my Facebook Page at divorce4u@facebook*
- *And our Facebook group: "Texas Law Public Discussion"*
- *And see videos and subscribe to the "Laura D. Heard Law Firm Inc" channel on YouTube*
- *Contact me at Website: www.LDHeard.com*

Laura Heard at Bexar County Courthouse

Jacqueline Calvert Reyna Esq., Associate Attorney

Laura Heard, Marta Torres, Tonya Barton

Marta Torres, paralegal/office manager

Glossary Of Terms

Glossary One: Divorce Legal Terminology

Alimony - Money paid after divorce to the ex-spouse, usually to the ex-spouse who is a lower wage-earner. Texas was the last of the 50 states to allow this, and Texas law calls it "maintenance" rather than alimony.

Annulment - An annulment creates a situation that is legally as if the marriage never happened. The practical aspect is that there is no community property, and the parties are to be put back in the property ownership position that they were in prior to the marriage. A civil annulment is actually more difficult to prove than a divorce, and there are limited grounds. The parties must have never consummated the marriage or as soon as the basis for the annulment is discovered, the parties must cease to co-habitate. A legal annulment requires a lawsuit and a court order just like a divorce.

Community Property - All property earned or acquired during the marriage is presumed to be community property, unless it is proven to be separate property. The name on the title is not controlling in this regard. No matter who earned the money or purchased the item, if the acquisition occurred during the marriage and it is community property, then the property is owned by both spouses. Texas courts may divide community property in whatever manner the court finds to be fair, not necessarily fifty-fifty.

Joint Managing Conservators - The law in Texas presumes that all fit parents should be appointed as Joint Managing Conservators of their children. Although the time with the child and decision-making powers are more equal, generally there is still only one Joint Managing

Conservator with the exclusive right to determine where the child resides, and the right to collect child support.

Managing Conservator - A parent or similar person who has, because of a court order, the right to possession of the child and extensive parental decision-making powers, including the right to determine where the child resides. This is the person who is usually referred to as having "custody" or "primary custody"

"No Fault" Grounds - There are several "grounds" or legal reasons for divorce, but the most popular is the "no fault" ground or insupportability, which provides that the marriage has become insupportable due to a conflict of personalities.

Possessory Conservator - A parent or similar person who has, because of a court order, the right to visitation with the child, but has less parental decision-making power.

Separate Property - Separate Property in Texas is any property owned prior to the marriage or acquired by gift or inheritance or due to personal injury at any time. However, the burden of proof is on the person claiming separate property to show proof that the property is not community property. Once found by a court to be separate, the court must award to the owner his or her own separate property.

Spousal Support - Refers to money or payments for the financial support of a spouse, court-ordered to be made while the parties are still married, but during the pendency of a divorce. While Texas does not favor post-divorce maintenance or alimony, Texas does prefer spousal support as needed because spouses have a legal duty to provide for the well-being of one another while they are married.

****

Glossary Two: <u>Legal Terminology for Estate Planning and Probate</u>

Decedent - A person who has died. A dead person. The deceased.

Deed - A document that is used as evidence of the ownership of an interest in real estate or as a way to transfer title in real estate.

Descendant – A blood relative who is of a younger generation in a direct line. Children, grandchildren, great-grandchildren, and so on.

Directive to Physicians – A document whereby the maker instructs his or her physician regarding whether or not to administer various types of life support in case the need arises. Also called a "living will" or an "advance directive."

Estate - The total of a person's assets, whether that person is alive or has died. The Estate may consist of both real and personal property, separate and community property. In the case of a decedent, it is the total interest in all property owned by the decedent at the moment of death, prior to distribution after death.

Execute - sign, finish, carry out

Executor / Executrix - A person named in a Will and approved by a Court who is in charge of gathering all the assets of the decedent's estate and managing the claims of creditors of the estate, and accomplishing the legal directives given in the Will including distributing the property to the beneficiaries named in the Will. The suffix of "-trix" indicates a female, but modern usage is to call both male and female an Executor.

Guardian - A person appointed by the Court with the right and duty to manage another living person's property for that person's benefit and/or to manage the person's care and well-being. Guardianship cannot be conferred without a court proceeding to determine that it is necessary. A guardian may be necessary because of physical, mental, or legal disability such that the person cannot manage their own business. Most commonly, a person may need a guardian because they have not yet reached the age of legal majority or a person of any age may need a guardian because of mental incapacity. A guardianship may be limited in scope or maybe temporary in time as the need dictates, but it always requires a court order after an evidentiary hearing to determine the need for the guardian and the guardian will have a bond requirement and strict oversight by the court.

Independent Executor - In Texas, a Will can specify that the Executor will act independently of the Court after the Executor is appointed. The word "Independent" is very important. This saves the Executor much time and money because the duties of the Executor can be performed without bond or Court oversight, but it also means that the person chosen as Independent Executor should be someone trustworthy.

Inter vivos - "from one living person to another living person"; Such as an inter vivos trust is one set up to transfer management and benefits of property from one person to another during the grantor's lifetime. An inter vivos trust is a living trust. It may or may not be revocable.

Intestate/Intestacy - meaning "without a will," refers to an estate of a deceased person who died without making a will.

Letters Testamentary - A certificate from the clerk of the Court that certifies that the named person has been appointed by the Court as Executor of a particular estate and that an order has been signed finding the Will to be legally valid ("admitting the Will to probate"), and that the Executor has qualified for the office by taking their Oath. Provides proof of the legal authority to act on behalf of the estate.

Letters of Administration - A certificate issued by the probate court that certifies that the named person has been appointed by the Court as Administrator of a particular intestate estate or one where the named executor is not to be appointed, and also that the Administrator has qualified for the office by taking an Oath and posting bond. Equal to Letters Testamentary evidencing the appointment of an Executor, but indicates that there was no appointment in a Will.

Letters of Guardianship - A certificate issued by the probate court that certifies the named person is the court-appointed guardian for a particular person known as a ward or guardian for the ward's estate.

Living Trust - See *inter vivos* trust above. A trust created and funded during life to manage property beginning during the lifetime of the maker.

Living Will- See Directive to Physicians. This is a non-legal term for a directive to physicians and is not a true Will since it does not distribute an estate.

LLC - Abbreviation for "Limited Liability Company." A legal business entity, similar to a corporation, but instead of stockholder owners, it has members and may be taxed differently, among other statutory differences. Primarily formed to shield the owners from business liabilities and debts, as well as to establish voting rights.

Muniment of Title - meaning "evidence of ownership." A muniment of title does not actually pass ownership such as to transfer ownership of land, but it may be used in certain instances as documentary evidence that the person named in the muniment is entitled to be treated as the owner. This is a process sometimes used to file a Will in the Deed records as evidence of the ownership in land without administering an estate.

Per capita - literally "by the head," referring to a system of determining the portion of an estate that a particular beneficiary will receive by counting the total number of individuals and dividing by that number so that every person gets an equal share regardless of their relationship to the decedent, share and share alike. Contrast to "per stirpes."

Per stirpes- literally "by the stem or root," referring to a system of determining the portion of an estate that a particular beneficiary will receive by first determining the level of relationship of the beneficiary, and then if a group has received the right to take a portion of an estate due to the death of a predecessor member, then only the portion that the original deceased member would have taken is divided equally among the next generation recipients. For example, grandchildren will divide only the portion that their parent would have taken if the parent had survived the decedent. The generation closest to the decedent keeps their original percentages, but the next generation divides one portion into smaller percentages. In contrast to "per capita."

Personal Property – any property that is not real estate. In other words, it could be cash, stocks, jewelry, electronics, or any other property except land and things attached to the land.

Power of Attorney - The document that appoints an agent to act on another living person's behalf and for that person's benefit. The power may be general or limited. There are powers of attorney to enable an agent to make medical decisions for another person, and other powers of attorney to enable an agent to make financial decisions. The power is automatically revoked upon the death of the principal (the person who gave the agent the power).

Probate - The process of court approval for managing a person's estate, whether the person is living (guardianship) or died with a Will (testate) or died without a Will (intestate). There are special courts designated to handle probate matters (probate court). A Will may be "admitted to probate" meaning that the court has approved the Will as a valid legal document.

Real Property - Land or real estate, including things attached to the land, such as a fence, home, or building. If it is not "real" property, then it is "personal" property.

Rule Against Perpetuities - A common law principle used in connection with a trust or instrument which transfers title to a property at a later time. The rule states that the conveyance is void if the title does not mandatorily vest within 21 years, plus a gestational period, after the death of a person existing at the time the interest was created. The rule has been modified in some cases by statute and has many interpretations.

Small Estate Affidavit - A special procedure in Texas wherein under extremely limited circumstances an intestate estate worth less than $75,000 may bypass normal intestacy requirements, but there are several statutory requisites, and the Court must approve the affidavit. The value of the estate is not the only consideration. The process can only be used where no administration of the estate is needed since no administrator will be appointed in this process, therefore no debts are owed by the estate other than the mortgage on the homestead, like a muniment of title, it doesn't truly transfer title but is merely evidence, and the estate cannot own real estate other than the decedent's homestead. The process is only for decedents' estates when there is no Will, and it only works for limited types of heirs.

Snowflake Embryo Adoption - Adoption of a frozen human embryo to be implanted in a non-biological parent.

Testator / Testatrix - A person who has made a Will. A testator may be a male or a generic person; Testatrix refers specifically to a female person who has made a Will.

Testamentary - pertaining to a Will or testament. A testament was historically only for passing personal property, while a will was for real estate, but in modern usage, a will is used for both real and personal property.

Testamentary Trust – A trust that is created by a Will to be formed and funded after the maker's death.

Trust - A right or management of property held by one person for the benefit of another. A person or institution known as the "trustee" is appointed by the maker and given the responsibility to manage the trust property according to the terms of the trust for the benefit of the beneficiary or beneficiaries. The trustee has an extremely high duty to safeguard the property for the beneficiaries and to follow the terms of the trust. The trust itself owns the property until the property passes out of the trust.

Will - A legal directive, usually a document, which determines what is to happen to a person's estate after they die. The Will has no effect until after the maker dies and the Court has determined that it complies with state probate law. It is revocable prior to the death of the maker. The state statutes are strictly interpreted to determine whether the Will is valid.

Laura D. Heard and the LDH Law Firm Team in 2022

****

INDEX

D

E

F

G

M

N

O

P

Notes

Made in the USA
Monee, IL
05 November 2026

67385031R10144